The Way of Peace

READINGS FOR A HARMONIOUS LIFE

Other titles in this series:

The Way of Peace

READINGS FOR
A HARMONIOUS LIFE

Michael Leach, Doris Goodnough,
Maria Angelini, editors

ORBIS BOOKS
Maryknoll, New York 10545

Founded in 1970, Orbis Books endeavors to publish works that enlighten the mind, nourish the spirit, and challenge the conscience. The publishing arm of the Maryknoll Fathers and Brothers, Orbis seeks to explore the global dimensions of the Christian faith and mission, to invite dialogue with diverse cultures and religious traditions, and to serve the cause of reconciliation and peace. The books published reflect the views of their authors and do not represent the official position of the Maryknoll Society. To learn more about Orbis Books, please visit our website at www.orbisbooks.com.

Library of Congress Cataloging-in-Publication Data

Names: Leach, Michael, 1940- editor. | Goodnough, Doris, editor. | Angelini, Maria, editor.

Title: The way of peace : readings for a harmonious life / Michael Leach, Doris Goodnough, Maria Angelini, editors.

Description: Maryknoll, NY : Orbis Books, [2020] | Includes bibliographical references and index. | Summary: "Divided into Peace of Heart, Peace on Earth, and Prayers for Peace, this anthology seeds peace in the family, the community, the nation, and the world"— Provided by publisher.

Identifiers: LCCN 2020048719 | ISBN 9781626984165 (paperback)

Subjects: LCSH: Peace—Religious aspects—Christianity. | Harmony (Philosophy)—Religious aspects—Christianity.

Classification: LCC BV4647.P35 W39 2020 | DDC 248.4—dc23

LC record available at https://lccn.loc.gov/2020048719

Peace I leave with you, my peace I give to you.
I do not give as the world gives.
So let not your hearts be troubled,
and do not be afraid.

—JOHN 14:27

Contents

THE WAY OF PEACE

Contents

Contents

Contents

Contents

Contents

Contents

THE WAY OF PEACE

Contents

THE WAY OF PEACE

Introduction

Dr. Thomas Hora, a psychiatrist who taught that problems are psychological but solutions are spiritual, once asked his class, "What is the essential spiritual value parents must foster in a home for their children to thrive?"

Hands raised. "Love!" said one of the students.

Another added: "Saint Paul said there are three essential virtues. Faith, hope, and love. And the greatest of these is love."

The others agreed. "Love makes the world go 'round," said one. "Love is all there is."

"Can you sing it for us?" the psychiatrist asked. The class laughed. Then the psychiatrist asked, "Can anyone think of a quality that must be present in a home *before* love can be either given or received?"

The students were puzzled. A spiritual value before love?

"Would you like to know?" asked the teacher.

They nodded.

"It is peace."

The students were silent. Some nodded.

"Without peace there is discord," the teacher said. "Conflict. Even hostility. Nothing good or beautiful can come without peace."

This is a book about peace. The peace that begins within ourselves and, like love, extends itself to others: the family, the community, the nation, the church, the earth. "Not peace as the world gives" (Jn 14: 27) but "the peace that is beyond understanding" (Phil 4: 7), the peace that "makes all things new" (Rev 21: 5).

The premise of this book is that peace of heart extends itself to peace on earth—and that none of this is possible without God.

Part One sets the table with stories, poems, and practices that help us cultivate inner peace. "We can never obtain peace in the world if we neglect the inner world and don't make peace with ourselves," writes the Dalai Lama. "World peace must develop out of inner peace."

Part Two focuses on individuals from all walks of life who have spread that peace to their communities and to the world. Being interested in peace and becoming an instrument of peace are inseparable. "If one is authentic," writes Sister Pat Farrell, OFM, "it leads to the other."

Part Three offers prayers from all faith traditions that plant seeds of peace, in ourselves and in our world. Theologian and novelist C. S. Lewis writes, "God can't give us peace and happiness apart from himself because there is no such thing."

Not everyone is called to give up their life for peace as Jesus did, or to work tirelessly for peace as Gandhi did. But each of us can perform life-changing little things that eighth-grader Riva Maendel suggests in her essay, blessings that bring benevolence into the world. "Do your little bit of good where you are," writes Archbishop Desmond Tutu. "It's those little bits of good put together that overwhelm the world."

And each of us can pray for peace wherever we are.

Our favorite prayer is to close our eyes and be still—"Be still and know that I am God" (Ps 46: 10)—and then think of someone we know who needs peace, or think of people we don't know who are desperate for peace, and pray with the voice of our soul, "I give you *my* peace. All my peace I give to *you*. All of it." Silently we repeat. An alchemy happens. The more peace we give, the more we receive. Our well empties and fills once again to overflowing. It is the way of peace. Try it. You'll like it.

The Way of Peace is the fifth book in a series that also includes *The Way of Kindness*, *The Way of Gratitude*, *The Way of Forgiveness,* and *The Way of Suffering*. The purpose of the series is to reassure you that spiritual values like kindness, gratitude, forgiveness, and peace reap tremendous benefits, and to offer you some inspiration for the journey. We editors have a long way to go on this bumpy path ourselves. That's why we have chosen as our spiritual companions, and now yours, some of the wisest individuals we know or could find. We're grateful you have chosen to stand by us on this journey. We give you all our peace. All of it.

MICHAEL LEACH
DORIS GOODNOUGH
MARIA ANGELINI

PART ONE

PEACE OF HEART

Everyone knows that peace has to begin with oneself, but not many people know how to do it.

—THICH NHAT HANH

Perfect Peace

Unknown

There once was a King who offered a prize to the artist who would paint the best picture of peace. Many artists tried. The King looked at all the pictures, but there were only two he really liked and he had to choose between them.

One picture was of a calm lake. The lake was a perfect mirror for peaceful towering mountains were all around it. Overhead was a blue sky with fluffy white clouds. All who saw this picture thought that it was a perfect picture of peace.

The other picture had mountains too. But these were rugged and bare. Above was an angry sky from which rain fell, in which lightning played. Down the side of the mountain tumbled a foaming waterfall. This did not look peaceful at all.

But when the King looked, he saw behind the waterfall a tiny bush growing in a crack in the rock. In the bush a mother bird had built her nest. There, in the midst of the

rush of angry water, sat the mother bird on her nest . . .
perfect peace.

Which picture do you think won the prize?

The King chose the second picture.

Do you know why?

"Because," explained the King, "peace does not mean to
be in a place where there is no noise, trouble, or hard work.
Peace means to be in the midst of all those things and still
be calm in your heart. That is the real meaning of peace."

*I have told you all this so that you may have "peace" in
me. Here on earth you will have many trials and sorrows.
But take heart, because I have overcome the world.* (John
16:33, NLT)

The Music of Silence

Brother David Steindl-Rast

Stopping at high noon for a moment of reflection is a spontaneous gesture of human consciousness. I remember when Tetsugen Glassman Sensei was being ordained the Abbot of Riverside Zendo in New York. It was a grand affair. Zen teachers from all over the country were gathered together to celebrate the event, with candles and incense and white chrysanthemums and black and gold brocade garments. In the middle of this solemn celebration, the beeper on somebody's wristwatch suddenly went off. Everybody was surreptitiously looking around to find the poor guy to whom this had happened, because generally you are not even supposed to wear a wristwatch in the Zendo. To everybody's surprise, the new Abbot himself interrupted the ceremony and said, "This was my wristwatch, and it was not a mistake. I have made a vow that regardless of what I am doing, I will interrupt it at noon and will think thoughts of peace." And then he invited everyone there to think thoughts of peace for a world that needs it.

Seven Practices for Peace

Deepak Chopra

The program for peacemakers asks you to follow a specific practice every day, each one centered on the theme of peace.

Our hope is that you will create peace on every level of your life. Each practice takes only a few minutes. You can be as private or outspoken as you wish. But those around you will know that you are for peace, not just through good intentions but by the way you conduct your life on a daily basis.

Sunday: Being for Peace

Today, take five minutes to meditate for peace. Sit quietly with your eyes closed. Put your attention on your heart and inwardly repeat these four words: Peace, Harmony, Laughter, Love. Allow these words to radiate from your heart's stillness out into your body.

As you end your meditation, say to yourself, Today I will relinquish all resentments and grievances. Bring into your mind anyone against whom you have a grievance and let it go. Send that person your forgiveness.

Monday: Thinking for Peace

Thinking has power when it is backed by intention. Today, introduce the intention of peace in your thoughts. Take a few moments of silence, then repeat this ancient prayer.

> Let me be loved, let me be happy, let me be peaceful.
> Let my friends by happy, loved, and peaceful.
> Let my perceived enemies be happy, loved, and peaceful.
> Let all beings be happy, loved, and peaceful.
> Let the whole world experience these things.

If at any time during the day you are overshadowed by fear or anger, repeat these intentions. Use this prayer to get back on center.

Tuesday: Feeling for Peace

This is the day to experience the emotions of peace. The emotions of peace are compassion, understanding, and love. Compassion is the feeling of shared suffering. When you feel someone else's suffering, there is the birth of understanding.

Understanding is the knowledge that suffering is shared by everyone. When you understand that you aren't alone in your suffering, there is the birth of love.

When there is love there is the opportunity for peace.

As you practice, observe a stranger some time during your day. Silently say to yourself, This person is just like me. Like me, this person has experienced joy and sorrow, despair and hope, fear and love. Like me, this person has people in his or her life who deeply care and love him or her. Like me, this person's life is impermanent and will one day end. This person's peace is as important as my peace. I want peace, harmony, laughter, and love in his or her life and the life of all beings.

Wednesday: Speaking for Peace

Today, the purpose of speaking is to create happiness in the listener. Have this intention: Today every word I utter will be chosen consciously. I will refrain from complaints, condemnation, and criticism.

Your practice is to do at least one of the following:

Tell someone how much you appreciate them.

Express genuine gratitude to those who have helped and loved you.

Offer healing or nurturing words to someone who needs them.

Show respect to someone whose respect you value.

If you find that you are reacting negatively to anyone, in a way that isn't peaceful, refrain from speaking and keep silent. Wait to speak until you feel centered and calm, and then speak with respect.

Thursday: Acting for Peace

Today is the day to help someone in need: a child, a sick person, an older or frail person. Help can take many forms. Tell yourself, Today I will bring a smile to a stranger's face. If someone acts in a hurtful way to me or someone else, I will respond with a gesture of loving kindness. I will send an anonymous gift to someone, however small. I will offer help without asking for gratitude or recognition.

Friday: Creating for Peace

Today, come up with at least one creative idea to resolve a conflict, either in your personal life or your family circle or among friends. If you can, try and create an idea that applies to your community, the nation, or the whole world. You may change an old habit that isn't working, look at someone a new way, offer words you never offered before, or think of an activity that brings people together in good feeling and laughter.

Secondly, invite a family member or friend to come up with one creative idea of this kind on his or her own. Creativity feels best when you are the one thinking up the new idea or approach. Make it known that you accept and enjoy creativity. Be loose and easy. Let the ideas flow and try out anything that has appeal. The purpose here is to bond, because only when you bond with others can there be mutual trust. When you trust, there is no need for hidden hostility and suspicion—the two great enemies of peace.

Saturday: Sharing for Peace

Today, share your practice of peacemaking with two people and invite them to begin the daily practice. As more of us participate in this sharing, our practice will expand into a critical mass.

Today, joyfully celebrate your own peace consciousness with at least one other peace-conscious person. Connect either through e-mail or phone.

Share your experience of growing peace.

Share your gratitude that someone else is as serious about peace as you are.

Share your ideas for helping the world move closer to critical mass.

Do whatever you can, in small or large ways, to assist anyone who wants to become a peacemaker.

There Are No Strangers

Thomas Merton

In Louisville, at the corner of Fourth and Walnut, in the center of the shopping district, I was suddenly overwhelmed with the realization that I loved all those people, that they were mine and I theirs, that we could not be alien to one another even though we were total strangers. It was like waking from a dream of separateness, of spurious self-isolation in a special world, the world of renunciation and supposed holiness. The whole illusion of a separate holy existence is a dream. Not that I question the reality of my vocation, or of my monastic life: but the conception of "separation from the world" that we have in the monastery too easily presents itself as a complete illusion: the illusion that by making vows we become a different species of being, pseudo-angels, "spiritual men," men of interior life, what have you.

It is a glorious destiny to be a member of the human race, though it is a race dedicated to many absurdities and one which makes many terrible mistakes: yet, with all that,

God Himself gloried in becoming a member of the human race. A member of the human race! To think that such a commonplace realization should suddenly seem like news that one holds the winning ticket in a cosmic sweepstake.

I have the immense joy of being man, a member of a race in which God Himself became incarnate. As if the sorrows and stupidities of the human condition could overwhelm me, now I realize what we all are. And if only everybody could realize this! But it cannot be explained. There is no way of telling people that they are all walking around shining like the sun.

This changes nothing in the sense and value of my solitude, for it is in fact the function of solitude to make one realize such things with a clarity that would be impossible to anyone completely immersed in the other cares, the other illusions, and all the automatisms of a tightly collective existence. My solitude, however, is not my own, for I see now how much it belongs to them—and that I have a responsibility for it in their regard, not just in my own. It is because I am one with them that I owe it to them to be alone, and when I am alone they are not "they" but my own self. There are no strangers!

Then it was as if I suddenly saw the secret beauty of their hearts, the depths of their hearts where neither sin nor desire nor self-knowledge can reach, the core of their reality, the person that each one is in God's eyes. If only they could all see themselves as they really are. If only we could see each other that way all the time. There would be no more war, no more hatred, no more cruelty, no more greed.

. . . I suppose the big problem would be that we would fall down and worship each other. But this cannot be seen, only believed and "understood" by a peculiar gift.

Pause for Peace

Slow down, you move too fast.
You got to make the morning last.

—Paul Simon

Never be in a hurry; do everything
quietly and in a calm spirit. Do not
lose your inner peace for anything
whatsoever, even if your whole world
seems upset.

—Saint Francis de Sales

Pause Practice

Pema Chödrön

Our habits are strong, so a certain discipline is required to step outside our cocoon and receive the magic of our surroundings. Pause practice—taking three conscious breaths at any moment when we notice that we are stuck—is a simple but powerful practice that each of us can do at any given moment.

Pause practice can transform each day of your life. It creates an open doorway to the sacredness of the place in which you find yourself. The vastness, stillness, and magic of the place will dawn upon you, if you let your mind relax and drop for just a few breaths the story line you are working so hard to maintain. If you pause just long enough, you can reconnect with exactly where you are, with the immediacy of your experience.

When you are waking up in the morning and you aren't even out of bed yet, even if you are running late, you could just look out and drop the story line and take three conscious breaths. Just be where you are! When you are washing up, or making your coffee or tea, or brushing your teeth, just create a gap in your discursive mind. Take three conscious breaths.

Just pause.

Let it be a contrast to being all caught up. Let it be like popping a bubble. Let it be just a moment in time, and then go on.

Maybe you are on your way to whatever you need to do for the day. You are in your car, or on the bus, or standing in line. But you can still create that gap by taking three conscious breaths and being right there with the immediacy of your experience, right there with whatever you are seeing, with whatever you are doing, with whatever you are feeling.

A Mindfulness Walk in Peace

John Dear

Mindfulness walking is a good exercise in the day-to-day practice of nonviolence. It forces us to slow down—literally—and to notice the trees, the bushes, the flowers, the sky and the birds, as well as to notice the resistance within us and how far short of "everyday peace" we fall.

Daily exercises in mindfulness help develop our patience, peaceableness, prayer and nonviolence. They not only reduce stress, but can open us to the simple joys of living. This is the flip side to our resistance to the culture of war. While we resist the culture of war and violence, we try to live every minute of every day in peace, hope and joy. One could argue that's too high a goal, but isn't that precisely the journey of the spiritual life? Why not try to reach for the heights and depths and horizons of peace?

"We walk slowly, in a relaxed way, keeping a light smile on our lips," Thich Nhat Hanh teaches in his writings about mindfulness walking. "When we practice this way, we feel deeply at ease, and our steps are those of the most secure person on Earth. All our sorrows and anxieties drop away, and peace and joy fill our hearts. Anyone can do it. It takes only a little time, a little mindfulness, and the wish to be happy."

He continues:

People say that walking on water is a miracle, but to me, walking peacefully on the earth is the real miracle. . . . Each step is a miracle. Taking steps on our beautiful planet can bring real happiness. As you walk, be fully aware of your foot, the ground, and the connection between them, which is your conscious breathing.

When we practice walking meditation, we arrive in each moment. Our true home is in the present moment. When we enter the present moment deeply, our regrets and sorrows disappear, and we discover life with all its wonders. Breathing in, we say to ourselves, "I have arrived." Breathing out we say, "I am home." When we do this, we overcome dispersion and dwell peacefully in the present moment, which is the only moment for us to be alive.

When the baby Buddha was born, he took seven steps, and a lotus flower appeared under each step. When you practice walking meditation, you can do the same. Visualize a lotus, a tulip or a gardenia blooming under each step the moment your foot touches the ground. If you practice beautifully like this, your friends will see fields of flowers everywhere you walk.

> If your steps are peaceful, the world will have
> peace. If you can make one peaceful step, then peace
> is possible. . . . Peace is every step.

Walking in mindful peace is like prayer, like communion. As far as the world is concerned, it is a waste of time. As far as heaven is concerned, it's a foretaste of the heavenly life to come.

We all experience this mindful walking when we process up the aisle in church to receive Holy Communion. In that moment, we are centered on Jesus. That holy experience summons us to live every moment in peace, mindfulness and communion with Jesus.

I think Jesus did everything nonviolently, mindfully and peacefully. He was perfectly centered, conscious and awake. He taught us to be peaceful and mindful ("Consider the lilies of the field. . . ." "Study the fig tree. . . ." "Notice the birds of the air. . . ."). He certainly taught, healed and walked with great grace and presence of mind. He was peaceful and mindful throughout his actions, conversations, civil disobedience and death, and certainly in his resurrection, when he breathed on the disciples. In light of Buddhist teachings, walking meditation helps us breathe in the breath of the risen Christ, that we might live in the Holy Spirit of peace.

Anyone who cares about humanity and the earth, who works for justice and peace, who resists injustice and war needs to take special care to practice the art of peace so we don't get swallowed whole by this violent culture of mindlessness. Daily peaceful living is essential if we are to offer the gift of peace to others. But what we're rarely told is how blessed the life of peace can be.

"The God of peace is never glorified by human violence," Thomas Merton once wrote. What Merton forgot to add is that the God of peace is always glorified by human nonviolence. Like Thomas Merton and Thich Nhat Hanh, let's continue to walk the path of peace in the fullness of peace that our lives might offer a gift of peace to others.

The Miracle Is to Walk on Earth

Thich Nhat Hanh

We do not have to die to enter the Kingdom of Heaven. In fact we have to be fully alive. When we breathe in and out and hug a beautiful tree, we are in Heaven. When we take one conscious breath, aware of our eyes, our heart, our liver, and our non-toothache, we are transported to Paradise right away. Peace is available. We only have to touch it. When we are truly alive, we can see that the tree is part of Heaven, and we are also part of Heaven. The whole universe is conspiring to reveal this to us, but we are so out of touch that we invest our resources in cutting down the trees. If we want to enter Heaven on Earth, we need only one conscious step and one conscious breath. When we touch peace, everything becomes real. We become ourselves, fully alive in the present moment, and the tree, our child, and everything else reveal themselves to us in their full splendor.

"The miracle is to walk on Earth." This statement was made by Zen Master Lin Chi. The miracle is not to walk on thin air or water, but to walk on Earth. The Earth is so beautiful. We are beautiful also. We can allow ourselves to walk mindfully, touching the Earth, our wonderful mother, with each step. We don't need to wish our friends, "Peace be with you." Peace is already with them. We only need to help them cultivate the habit of touching peace in each moment.

Pause for Peace

All we do our whole lives is go from one little piece of Holy Ground to the next.

—SEYMOUR GLASS

A deep peace floods the soul, transitory things are nothing. We are walking toward God, contemplating his immense happiness and rejoicing forever in the thought of the infinite, perfect, unchangeableness happiness of this God we love; we are happy with the happiness of the Beloved, and the thought of his unchangeable peace calms the soul.

—CHARLES DE FOUCAULD

There lies the dearest freshness deep down things.

—GERARD MANLEY HOPKINS

Dandelions

Michael Leach

Jesus taught us to be at peace by beholding God in the birds of the air and the lilies of the field. I once said a Mass for children who were sitting in a field of dandelions next to a lake with frogs popping out like Muppets. I read the gospel on the flowers of the field and then asked the children: "Each one of you, go and choose a flower and just look at it." They scattered and each found a pet dandelion and put their face close to it. "Just look at it," I said. "And see how it grows." The children smiled as the yellow lions smiled back. I waited. I whispered, "If I could look into your eyes right now, I would see a flower. God is everywhere, and each of you is baptizing a flower."

Shortest sermon I ever gave.

Trees, Sister Trees

Dom Hélder Câmara

Ah, trees,
do you live in peace,
in harmony,
despite the differences
between you
which to the human eye
seem so immense?
How do you feel,
you towering palms,
you massive oaks,
you giant baobabs,
as you stare down upon
a tiny bush?
Are the fruit bearers,
apple, mango, and coconut,
tempted to mock
those who have simply
leaves and thorns?

Do you welcome
the birds' nests
and children who swing
from your branches?
What is it like
when the leaves fall
and your branches are draped
in snow?
Does spring give a hint
of the thought of resurrection?
And what is it like when
drought wounds the land
and you trees seem to raise
up your arms
in silent prayer
to our Lord and Father?
What do you feel
at the plucking of your fruits?
Is the stoning
the worst part?
And what is your pain
when your branches are pruned,
or when a tree entire
goes to the lumber yard
to be cut
into houses or bridges or chairs or beds?
Do you understand the purpose
of a bridge
and the vivid symbol it is?

Dom Hélder Câmara

Do you realize your importance in
the building of a home?
Chairs and beds
call to mind rest
and make us think
of the family:
But what does it mean to you?
When lightning strikes a tree,
is it true that the tree
prefers itself to be struck
than to see a person or house
destroyed?
Remember, sister Tree,
that the Son of God
in order to reconcile us
with our Father and his,
bore a heavy cross.
Three times he fell
under that burden,
and wanted to die
nailed to the cross
in order to save us.

10

The Peace of Wild Things

Wendell Berry

When despair for the world grows in me
And I wake in the night at the least sound
In fear of why my life and my children's
      lives may be,
I go and lie down where the wood drake
Rests in his beauty on the water, and the
      great heron feeds.
I come into the peace of wild things
who do not tax their lives with fore-
      thought
Of grief. I come into the presence of still
      water.
And I feel above me the day-blind stars
Waiting with their light. For a time
I rest in the grace of the world, and am
      free.

Pause for Peace

Meditation is not a way of making your mind quiet. It is a way of entering into the quiet that is already there— buried under the 50,000 thoughts the average person thinks every day.

—Deepak Chopra

You find peace not by rearranging the circumstances of your life but realizing who you are at the deepest level.

—Eckhart Tolle

Within you, there is a stillness and a sanctuary to which you can retreat at any time and be yourself.

—Hermann Hesse

The Way of Peace

He that dwelleth in the secret place of the most High shall abide under the shadow of the Almighty.

—Psalm 91

Remember, the entrance to the sanctuary is inside you.

—Rumi

11

The Cave of the Heart

Joan Chittister

The question is, then, what is the way to the beginning of peace?

The philosopher Blaise Pascal wrote, "The unhappiness of a person resides in one thing, to be unable to remain peacefully in a room." It is silence and solitude that bring us face to face with ourselves and the inner wars we must win if we are ever to become truly whole, truly at peace. Silence gives us the opportunity we need to raise our hearts and minds to something above ourselves, to be aware of a spiritual life in us that is being starved out by noise pollution, to still the raging of our limitless desires. It is a call to the Cave of the Heart where the vision is clear and the heart is centered on something worthy of it.

There are some things in life that deserve to be nourished simply for their own sake. Art is one, music is another, good reading is a third, but the power of the contemplative vision is the greatest of them all. Only those who come to see the world as God sees the world, only those who see through the eyes of God, ever really see the glory of the world, ever really approach the peaceable kingdom, ever find peace in themselves.

Silence is the beginning of peace. It is in silence that we learn that there is more to life than life seems to offer. There is beauty and truth and vision wider than the present and deeper than the past that only silence can discover. Going into ourselves we see the whole world at war within us and begin to end the conflict. To understand ourselves, then, is to understand everyone else as well.

Because we have come to know ourselves better, we can only deal more gently with others. Knowing our own struggles, we reverence theirs. Knowing our own failures, we are in awe of their successes, less quick to condemn, less likely to boast, less intent on punishing, less certain of our certainties, less committed to our heady, vacuous, and untried convictions. Then silence becomes a social virtue.

Make no doubt about it, the ability to listen to another, to sit silently in the presence of God, to give sober heed and to ponder is the nucleus of the spirituality of peace. It may, in fact, be what is most missing in a century saturated with information, sated with noise, smothered in struggle, but short on reflection. The Word we seek is speaking in the silence within us. Blocking it out with the static of nonsense day in and day out, relinquishing the spirit of silence, anesthetizes the heart in a noise-numbed world and destroys our peace.

An ancient wrote: "Once upon a time a disciple asked the elder, 'How shall I experience my oneness with creation?'"

And the elder answered, "By listening."

The disciple pressed the point: "But how am I to listen?"

And the elder taught, "Become an ear that pays attention to every single thing the universe is saying. The moment you hear something you yourself are saying, stop."

Peace will come when we stretch our minds to listen to the noise within us that needs quieting and the wisdom from outside ourselves that needs to be learned. Then we will have something of value to leave the children besides hate, besides war, besides turmoil. Then peace will come. Then we will be able to say with Kazantzakis, "I fear nothing. I hope for nothing. I am free."

There Is a Place in You

A Course in Miracles

There is a place in you where
this whole world has been forgotten,
where no memory of sin and of illusion
    lingers still.
There is a place in you which time has
    left,
and echoes of eternity are heard.
There is a resting place so still
no sound except a hymn to Heaven
    rises up
to gladden God the Father and the Son.
Where Both abide are They remem-
    bered, Both.
And where They are is Heaven and is
    peace.

Peace in the World Cannot Be Made without Peace in the Heart

Henri J. M. Nouwen

Although the remark "Change the world, begin with yourself" has often been used to individualize or spiritualize the urgent task of bringing peace to our planet, it points to the undeniable truth that peace in the world cannot be made without peace in the heart.

This is beautifully illustrated by a little story found in the tales of the Desert Fathers.

There were three friends who were eager workers, and one of them chose to devote himself to making peace between people who were fighting in accordance with "Blessed are the peacemakers." The second chose to visit the sick. The third went off to live in tranquillity in the desert. The first toiled away at the quarrels of men, but could not resolve them all, and so he went to the one who was looking after the sick, and he found him flagging too, not succeeding in fulfilling the commandment. So the two of them agreed to go and visit the one who was living in the desert. They told him of their difficulties and asked him to tell them what he had been able to do. He was silent for a time, then he poured water into a bowl and said to them, "Look at the water." It was all turbulent. A little later he told them to look at it again, and see how the water had settled down. When they looked at it, they saw their own faces as in a mirror. Then he said to them, "In the same way a person who is living in the midst of people does not see his own sins because of all the disturbance, but if he becomes tranquil, especially in the desert, then he can see his own shortcomings." (Benedicta Ward, *The Wisdom of the Desert Fathers*)

This story leaves little doubt that tranquility of the heart is not a way to "feel good" while the world is ripped apart by violence and war, but a way to come in touch with our being part of the problem. Prayer leads to spiritual tranquility and spiritual tranquility leads us to the confession of our sins, the sins that lead to war. Making peace between people and visiting the sick are important, but doing these things without a repentant heart cannot bear fruit. When we can see our own sinful self in a tranquil mirror and confess that we too are warmakers, then we may be ready to start walking humbly on the road to peace.

Pause for Peace

*The most beautiful thing a man can do
is forgive wrong.*

—JUDAISM

*Then Peter came up to him and said,
"Lord, how often shall my brother sin
against me, and I forgive him? As many
as seven?" Jesus said to him, "I do not
say to you seven times, but seventy
times seven."*

—CHRISTIANITY

Forgive thy servants seventy times a day.

—ISLAM

*To forgive is the highest, most beautiful
form of love. In return, you will receive
untold peace and happiness.*

—ROBERT MULLER

The Way of Peace

When I am able to resist the temptation to judge others, I can see them as teachers of forgiveness in my life, reminding me that I can only have peace of mind when I forgive rather than judge.

—GERALD JAMPOLSKY

Forgiveness equals inner peace—more peaceful people equals more world peace.

—RICHARD BRANSON

14

Pray for Peace

Amy Eilberg

Each of us received the same instructions—to silently offer wishes of well-being to a variety of people, using classical Buddhist phrases or words of our own. "May you be safe. May you be well. May you be happy. May you be at peace." On the first day we were to offer well wishes to ourselves, since cultivating our own reservoir of loving-kindness is what best enables us to develop kindness toward others. On the second day we were to offer the same hopes toward someone so beloved to us that the very thought of that person immediately makes us smile. As we developed increasingly powerful sensations of the power of loving-kindness in us, we moved toward wishing for the well-being of people that we hardly know and even to people who had hurt us, if and when we felt ready to do so, and ultimately, to all beings in the world.

Having been on such retreats before, I knew that the next step was to experiment with offering blessings to everyone in the room and eventually to everyone in our lives. I had heard a teacher suggest that we wish for the well-being of every person who crossed our path as we walked silently around the retreat center, on the way to or from lunch or the meditation hall. The moment I would see someone coming in the opposite direction on the path, I would silently recite, "May you be safe. May you be well. May you be happy. May you be at peace." I began to do the same for people who crossed the path of my thoughts. As someone in my life spontaneously floated into my awareness (a friend, a community member, an estranged family member, a despised political figure), I offered the phrases to that person as well. "May you be safe. May you be well. May you be happy. May you be at peace."

The practice was flowing through me. In those blessed moments and hours during which my concentration was strong and focused, I genuinely wanted the best—the basic blessings that I know all people desire—for everyone who crossed my path, either physically or imaginatively.

Then I noticed something really interesting. I realized that I felt as if I had gotten very fat, as if my belly and chest had filled up with loving-kindness. Then I realized that I felt happy. Very happy. That overstuffed feeling shifted into feeling full of joy. It was so wonderful, in that moment, to have kindly feelings toward everyone. It was something like the mysterious way in which helping another or giving a gift to another brings us joy. But I wasn't doing anything or giving anything. I was just walking around the retreat center, full of love for everyone.

Of course, the experience did not leave me in a permanent state of total love and kindness. Nor did it leave me with a craving to reproduce the experience on any particular schedule. It was a moment's experience that came and went, as all experiences do.

But I did leave with a powerful and precious memory to reflect on. As I thought about what had happened for me that day, the memory became a kind of prayer. Remembering that sensation of feeling full of love and joy for all the people in my life and for myself, I knew that this was the way I wanted to live, as much and as often as possible. I knew that this was what my work on peacebuilding is about: trying to bring a measure of kindness and blessing to everyone I encounter.

It is as simple and as challenging as this. The desire for the well-being of all people is what moves us to work for peace, and this same desire makes it possible for us to care for all people in any conflict. Though we may be more connected to one "side" or more inclined toward one viewpoint in the dispute, on a deeper level, we sense a bond of common humanity with everyone involved. We want what is best for all of them. Like a parent responding to estrangement among her children, she wants for all of them to be happy, for all of them to thrive, for all of them to be free of the pain of ruptured relationships.

This is what I wish for you and for all people who honor the cause of peace. I want for you to believe that it is a meaningful and attainable goal in our lives to touch the natural desire of our hearts to feel kindness, to embody caring in our relationships, in our communities, and in our world. I hope that this ground of kindheartedness toward all people will move you to bring a healing presence to conflict wherever you encounter it—from arguments in your family and workplace to deeply broken personal relationships in your life to connections of openhearted curiosity with people of religions and political views different from your own. I want your benevolent sense of caring for all who live on God's earth to move you to help ease pain and restore connection in the human family.

Most of us ordinary mortals cannot live this way all the time, but we can live this way some of the time, and surely that makes a difference. The more of us adopt this goal as an intention for our lives, the more peace and harmony there will be in the world.

Grant peace, goodness and blessing, grace, kindness, and compassion upon us and all Your people Israel. Bless us, our Parent, as one, with the light of Your face, for in Your light You have given us, O God, the Torah of life, love of kindness, justice, blessing, compassion, life, and peace. May it be good in Your sight to bless Your people Israel at all times and at every moment with Your peace. Blessed are You, God, who blesses the people Israel—and all the inhabitants of the earth—with peace.

This beautiful prayer, offered every morning of the Jewish year, and in a slightly different form in evening prayers as well, asks for God's blessings of peace upon us all. Strikingly, the prayer associates peace with a host of other blessings: grace, kindness, compassion, justice, and life itself. Perhaps in this prayer we are asking God for an array of separate blessings. Or perhaps, this text teaches that peace is inextricable from goodness, ease and well-being, justice, good health, and harmony. These are the blessings for which everyone longs.

Prayer for peace has become a central practice in my life. We cannot know how prayer works in the world. But I know that the more we pray for peace, goodness, health, harmony, and grace for all beings, the stronger will be the power of peace and kindness in the world.

Be this prayer, and take it with you wherever you go, every day. Know that you are part of an enormous circle of peace-seekers all over the world. May our prayers multiply, and may the actions that flow from our prayerful intentions help create a more peaceful world, the kind of world that God desires for all of us.

15

Peace Within through *Ubuntu*

Robert V. Taylor

The way of peace is about peace to the third power, peace within, between and among people. They are profoundly interconnected in creating lives of well-being. A life devoted to peace is sustained by cultivating your own inner peace. The African wisdom tradition of *Ubuntu* sheds light on our practices for nurturing peace within.

Ubuntu is often identified with people like Nelson Mandela and Desmond Tutu for the way in which their peacemaking was infused with delight and joy even amid horrific human enmity and violence.

This is the essence of *Ubuntu*. A person is only a person in the context of other people. I can only be my finest self if you are able to be your finest self. In other words, we need one another to discover our magnificence and allow it to shine.

It is a way of life that acknowledges the infinite value of every person regardless of creed, gender, nationality, or orientation. It replaces fear, hate and distrust with heartfelt curiosity, empathy, and generosity.

Active engagement with the world is what *Ubuntu* invites. Whenever the magnificence of others is confined, scorned, or dismissed you intuitively join others in actively seeking to expand your consciousness of what it means to be human. This naturally involves the pursuit of justice for all. It is a joyful choice for how to be human!

Here are three practices by which *Ubuntu* finds expression in creating peace within so that we can also create peace between and among people.

Be attentive to those around you. In the bustle of daily life it is common to take those around you for granted as a known quantity. You may admire, tolerate or be dismayed at people for qualities or behaviors they display. The ones who dismay or anger you will drain your spirit and energy if you cede them that power. Your bandwidth for engaging with others is a precious and limited resource. The choices of whom to surround yourself with will either detract from or enliven your inner peace.

Ubuntu invites you to live a life of curiosity about others. The Middle English derivation of the word is "cure," which is about restoring and healing. Curiosity about the stories, traditions, voices, and lives of others enlivens your imagination about the truth that we are only people because of one another.

Mindfully put your energy with those whose lives exhibit well-being for themselves and others. Create time to be together so you may glean truths and wisdom about nurturing peace within. Your mutual quest for peace within will radiate beyond the borders of your own life creating a rippling effect in the world.

Own your cluttered conversations. The things that clutter our lives tend to have a life of their own distracting us from inner peace. Old story lines and conversations rattling around inside of you are pernicious because of their toxicity. To be untethered from them requires setting yourself free from them.

These are the conversations that undermine your well-being by ensnaring you in their hurt, pain, betrayal, or fear. They detract you from knowing that peace within is possible. Naming and detaching from them and offering them to the care of the Universe is a liberating cleansing.

Each time you do this you become freer to pay attention to your unique personal story and the wisdom revealed by all the elements of it. To practice *Ubuntu* is to discover redemption and grace in your story. Attentiveness to it reveals that you are still shaping and forming your evolving story which invites you to appreciate and learn from the stories of others. New life-giving conversations become pathways to inner peace in the grittiness of human stories heard with your attentive ears.

Forgive instead of paying back. Research suggests that forgiveness is good for you! When you are unable to forgive someone, you harm yourself by allowing part of your life to be occupied by an egregious person. The person who harmed you gives little thought to you or what they did.

To forgive does not mean forgetting but it is a choice to be free.

I ran into someone whose malicious agenda against me disrupted my life in unexpected ways. Years ago, I chose to forgive him, and my life opened to new possibilities. But there he was professing to not know or recognize me. The unexpected encounter brought back memories of a traumatic experience. Would I allow him to reoccupy my life? I was reminded that the choice to forgive often presents itself repeatedly. A choice to experience freedom more profoundly.

Forgiveness expands your empathy which is the antithesis of enmity. Your empathy is a generator of interconnection with others and it is courageous because it is a choice to be aware of your unconscious biases and step beyond them. Empathy beckons you to honor the stories and lives of those you may not know or understand. Your forgiving empathetic self is an incubator of generous life.

With these practices for peace within experienced through the wisdom of *Ubuntu*, you turn away from settling for serial moments of peace within to choose a way that grounds your work of making the world a more hopeful and just place. Peace within you will be a blessing to many!

16

Nothing Can Separate Us from the Love of God

Michael Leach

> *Neither death nor life, nor angels nor*
> *principalities nor powers, nor things*
> *present nor things to come, nor height*
> *nor depth, nor any other created thing,*
> *shall be able to separate us from the*
> *love of God which is in Christ Jesus*
> *our Lord!*

—ROMANS 8:38–39

What could bring us more peace? No matter what we do or how bad we think we are, nothing can separate us from the love of God. How could it? "We live and move and have our being in God" (Acts 17:28). Can anyone separate a wave from the ocean or a sunbeam from the sun? We are spiritual beings made of the same stuff as our Creator. God can no more remove us than we can remove God.

Jesus assures us: "I am in my Father, and you in me, and I in you. God will never leave you!" (John 14:20). When Jesus saved the adulteress about to be stoned, he didn't say, "Sin no more and I will not condemn you." He said, "I do not condemn you. *Now* go and sin no more." We first experience God's love, and *then* our life changes forever. Can any experience bring us more peace, in an instant, than this one?

I saw a beautiful demonstration of the truth that "nothing can separate us from the love of God" at a religious convention many years ago. Late at night I took the hotel elevator to a floor where the host organization had a hospitality suite for the conference speakers. People packed the room in clusters, ice crackling in cocktail glasses, smoke swirling from cigarettes. My eyes immediately went to the far corner of the room where a nun sat on a sofa, a thin young man resting his head on her chest. The Sister was Jeannine Gramick, a friend whose book on ministering to gays and lesbians in the church I had just published. The boy was so thin and he seemed so weary. I wondered: does he have AIDS? Jeannine touched his hair with her fingers, gently, like the feathers of an angel. I thought for a moment that someone had moved the Pieta from St. Peter's Basilica to this hotel on the outskirts of Chicago. I was aware that the institutional church did not go out of its way to embrace gay Catholics and I could not take my eyes off this Catholic Sister who was demonstrating—quietly, without fanfare, in the corner of a room—the basic

Christian truth that "nothing can separate us from the love of God—*nothing.*"

Just as nothing can separate us from the love of God, not death, not sin, not anything, nothing can separate us from each other. We are literally one with one another. This truth is the ground of all nonviolence. When Jesus said, "Love your neighbor as yourself," he meant it literally. We *are* our neighbor, and our neighbor is *us.* Jesus said, "I and my Father are one," and then went on to teach us how to pray by saying, "*Our* Father...." We are all, each of us, brothers and sisters, children of God, made in the image and likeness of love. What could bring us more peace?

Pause for Peace

Inner peace is letting go of being right.
—HUGH PRATHER

Don't let people pull you into their storm. Pull them into your peace.
—KIMBERLY JONES

Kindness is essential to inner peace.
—DALAI LAMA

A Native American grandfather was talking to his grandson about his feelings. He said, "I feel as if I have two wolves fighting in my heart. One wolf is vengeful, angry, and violent. The other wolf is peaceful, loving, and compassionate."

The grandson asked him, "Which wolf will win the fight in your heart?"

The grandfather answered, "The one I feed."

—Unknown

17

The Bell

Sister Annabel Laity

If there is one thing that belongs to global spirituality it is the sound of the bell. Throughout the world, the sound of the bell brings people back to the spiritual dimension.

Once I was standing in our Buddhist nunnery with two Catholic nuns. The monastery bell rang out, and I stopped talking. The two nuns were not surprised at all. They told me that in their convent the bell was rung every hour, and at that time all the nuns would stop what they were doing and recollect that they were in the presence of God.

How in our busy daily life can we have the opportunity to stop running and come back to the present moment? God is always present. It is we who have wandered off somewhere forgetting to be there for God.

When I was a child, the nuns in the convent school rang the Angelus bell at six in the morning, midday, and six in the evening. The whole school would gather at midday and recite the prayers. Moreover, every class began and ended with prayer. The intention was that the pupils' daily routines would be imbued with spirituality, but too often the prayers became an outer form with no real spiritual content. The secret is to be able to stop running. Our lives are made of a series of events, one leading into another, and often we just want to finish one thing in order to start another. We want to finish washing up in order to have a cup of tea, and then we want to finish the cup of tea in order to turn on the television. We never really stay with what we are doing in order to savor the present moment and be truly alive. If we are not careful, we shall want to finish saying the prayers so we can go and do something different.

The sound of the bell is an important part of the practice of mindfulness. It helps us stop our body, speech, and thinking from always running into the future or going back into the past. It helps us be truly present, with our body and mind no longer in two different places. The bell says, "Stop, breathe, and enjoy being alive."

Not all of us live near a church or a monastery. So we need ersatz bells. If you work on a computer, the sound of the bell can be downloaded using an app to help you stop and breathe mindfully every half hour or so. Your breathing will renew your body and mind. You can close your eyes and give all your attention to your in- and out-breath as you listen to the sound of the bell.

Every time your telephone rings, rather than answer straightaway, you can enjoy one, two, or three in- and out-breaths in order to be in the presence of God, before you reply, so that your voice on the phone will be reassuring and kind.

In Buddhism, we say the sound of the bell brings us back to our true home. In Christianity, we say the sound of the bell brings us into the presence of God. There is really no difference between the feeling of being at home in our body and mind and the feeling of being in the presence of God. They are just different words describing the same thing. Our conscious breathing is important to help us stop and be in the presence of God.

After a while whenever you hear a bell you will automatically come back to yourself and be aware of the breath in your body. In order to pray, our mind needs to be very still. So we can begin a session of prayer with the sound of the bell. Conscious breathing helps us still our mind and empty it of unnecessary thinking.

18

The Be It Poem

Doug Crandall

Tag.
You're it.
I just touched you with the peace baton
and now you have to be it
for a day.
Peace
that is
going one whole day
(an eternity)
forgiving all things
thoughts
which seem to transgress
upon you.
This task now yours
Enjoy your day
finding peace to be much more
heavenly

than the hell you are used to.
Pass it on!

PART TWO

PEACE ON EARTH

Blessed are the peacemakers,
for they will be called children of God.

—JESUS

19

Love Your Enemies

Jesus in Matthew 5:38–48

You have heard that it was said, "An eye for an eye, and a tooth for a tooth." But I tell you, do not violently resist an evil person. If anyone slaps you on the right cheek, turn to them the other cheek also. And if anyone wants to sue you and take your shirt, let them have your coat as well. If anyone forces you to go one mile, go with them two miles. Give to the one who asks you, and do not turn away from the one who wants to borrow from you.

You have heard that it was said, "You shall love your neighbor and hate your enemy." But I say to you, love your enemies and pray for those who persecute you, so that you may be sons of your Father who is in heaven; for He causes His sun to rise on the evil and the good, and sends rain on the righteous and the unrighteous. For if you love those who love you, what reward do you have? Do not even the tax collectors do the same? If you greet only your brothers, what more are you doing than others? Even

the Gentiles do that. Therefore, you must be all embracing,
just as your Father is all embracing.

20

The Magna Carta of Christian Nonviolence

Pope Benedict XVI

Love your enemies. . . . This Gospel passage is rightly considered the *magna carta* of Christian nonviolence. It does not consist of succumbing to evil, as a false interpretation of "turning the other cheek" (cf. Lk 6:29) claims, but in responding to evil with good (cf. Rom 12:17–21) and thereby breaking the chain of injustice.

One then understands that for Christians, nonviolence is not merely tactical behavior but a person's way of being, the attitude of one who *is so convinced of God's love and power* that he is not afraid to tackle evil with the weapons of love and truth alone.

Love of one's enemy constitutes the nucleus of the "Christian revolution," a revolution not based on strategies of economic, political or media power: the revolution of love, a love that does not rely ultimately on human resources but is a gift of God which is obtained by trusting solely and unreservedly in his merciful goodness. Here is the newness of the Gospel which silently changes the world! Here is the heroism of the "lowly" who believe in God's love and spread it, even at the cost of their lives.

21

The Good News

Pope Francis

Jesus lived in violent times. Yet he taught that the true battlefield, where violence and peace meet, is the human heart: for "it is from within, from the human heart, that evil intentions come" (Mk 7:21). But Christ's message in this regard offers a radically positive approach. He unfailingly preached God's unconditional love, which welcomes and forgives. He taught his disciples to love their enemies (cf. Mt 5:44) and to turn the other cheek (cf. Mt 5:39). When he stopped her accusers from stoning the woman caught in adultery (cf. Jn 8:1–11), and when, on the night before he died, he told Peter to put away his sword (cf. Mt 26:52), Jesus marked out the path of nonviolence. He walked that path to the very end, to the cross, whereby he became our peace and put an end to hostility (cf. Eph 2:14–16). Whoever accepts the Good News of Jesus is able to acknowledge the violence within and be healed by God's mercy, becoming in turn an instrument of reconciliation. In the words of Saint Francis of Assisi: "As you announce peace with your mouth, make sure that you have greater peace in your hearts."

To be true followers of Jesus today also includes embracing his teaching about nonviolence. As my predecessor Benedict XVI observed, that teaching "is realistic because it takes into account that in the world there is too much violence, too much injustice, and therefore that this situation cannot be overcome except by countering it with more love, with more goodness. This 'more' comes from God." He went on to stress that: "For Christians, nonviolence is not merely tactical behaviour but a person's way of being, the attitude of one who is so convinced of God's love and power that he or she is not afraid to tackle evil with the weapons of love and truth alone. Love of one's enemy constitutes the nucleus of the 'Christian revolution.'" The Gospel command to love your enemies (cf. Lk 6:27) "is rightly considered the Magna Carta of Christian nonviolence. It does not consist in succumbing to evil . . . , but in responding to evil with good (cf. Rom 12:17–21), and thereby breaking the chain of injustice."

22

It Starts with Us

Riva Maendel

With all the strength in my arm, I furiously slammed the door. On the other side, my sister was almost as mad as I was. In my opinion, she deserved getting hurt. Looking back, I am embarrassed that all this anger was about washing dishes, but that's how walls of hatred are built—one small brick at a time. Later, as I lay on my bed, I regretted my actions and thought about steps I could take to promote peace.

The pope gives me a good direction: he tells us to take a clear stand for creative and active nonviolence. I like that word, *creative*. Thinking back to my conflict with my sister, I realize that taking a nonviolent stand would have made

Riva Maendel, an eighth-grader at the Bruderhof community's Fox Hill School in Walden, New York, won the $1,000 Bishop Francis X. Ford Award, named for the Maryknoll priest who was in the first group of Maryknoll missioners to China and died in a prison there in 1952.

me so much happier. If I had offered to do the dishes for her, I would be promoting peace!

Our world is full of violence. There are people dying from drug overdoses, shootings, gang-related issues and war. I can't even begin to take a stand on these bigger issues if I fight my sister. So, my first small step is to apologize, and I realize what an amazing power two small words, "I'm sorry," can have.

Almost everyone in the world wants peace, but we don't know how to find it. One way to bring peace is by praying. We need to pray every day for peace—in our hearts, in our families, in our schools, communities, churches and the entire world. I think of all the Christians in the Middle Eastern countries who are dying for their faith. These Christians risk their lives to bring the message of peace and nonviolence to those in the Middle East. I also worry about the nuclear standoff that we have with North Korea. I pray that our country will find a peaceful solution to this issue. Another thing that bothers me is the escalation of shootings in our country. We need to pray for all those mourning the loss of loved ones. They are in desperate need of peace.

Before we can achieve peace on an international level, we must work toward attaining peace in our daily relationships with those closest to us. I will probably never get a chance to put my life on the line like the Christians in the Middle East. I pray that my school never experiences a school shooting, but nonetheless, I can take a stand for peace and nonviolence every day. I can show my convictions in the small things I do each day. Respecting my parents is promoting peace. Helping out with chores in my house and avoiding conflict with my sister are definite ways to promote peace. At school, the way I interact with my peers will influence the younger students in our school. I can also show interest and support the local organizations in my community that work for peace: our local police officers, AA and other organizations that work towards bringing peace to those who are trapped in a cycle of violence. Even though our efforts might seem small and insignificant, we are actively working for peace.

As we strive for peace, we must remember how important forgiveness is. When we forgive, we can learn to trust. Every little block of peace will help build the foundation for future generations.

Blessed Are the Peacemakers

Clarence Jordan

Yes, the pure in heart shall see God in his Word, which they will understand as never before. They shall see him in his work, which had been a perplexing riddle to them. They shall see him in his holy temple, the new Israel, the Christian fellowship. But they not only shall see him, they shall be like him. "The peacemakers are partakers of the divine blessing, for they shall be called children of God."

It is the Father's nature to make peace. He is called the God of peace. His Son was called the Prince of peace. Paul says, "He is our peace." The consuming desire of God seems to have been voiced by the angels at the birth of his Son: "... on earth, peace!"

So God is a peacemaker. Quite naturally, little peacemakers, bearing his image, "shall be called children of God." The final step causes the newborn child to be recognized as a true son or daughter, having been begotten of God.

But what is peacemaking? We aren't sure of all that it means, but we can safely say, "It's what God does." And the

Bible portrays God as bent on one thing—the salvation of the world. So we might conclude that a peacemaker is one who identifies with God in the plan of redeeming the world. In this way it becomes a parent-child business with a common objective.

With Jesus, peacemaking involved not merely a change of environment, but also a change of heart. God's plan of making peace is not merely to bring about an outward settlement between evil people, but to create people of goodwill.

When Jesus proclaimed the kingdom of God on earth, he was not offering to make people more comfortable in their sins. He was calling them to a new life in the spirit and to citizenship in his beloved community, which alone is capable of peace. The peacemakers, then, are the agents of the kingdom of heaven. Their assignment is to make "the kingdom of the world become the kingdom of our Lord, and of his Christ" (Rev. 11:15).

Pause for Peace

Those who see all creatures within themselves and themselves within all creatures know no fear. Those who see all creatures in themselves and them-selves in all creatures know no grief. How can the multiplicity of life delude the one who sees its unity?

—HINDUISM (ISHA UPANISHAD 6–7)

Love your neighbor as yourself.

—JUDAISM (LEVITICUS 19:18)

This is my commandment, that you love one another as I have loved you.

—CHRISTIANITY (JOHN 15:12)

Not one of you is a believer until he loves for his brother what he loves for himself.

—ISLAM (FORTY HADITH OF AN-NAWAWI 13)

76

Pause for Peace

Sane and insane, all are searching love-
lorn for God, in mosque, temple, church,
alike. For only God is the One God of
Love, and Love calls from all these, each
one to God's home.

—SUFISM

The Eternal Law of Love

Mohandas Gandhi

Though I cannot claim to be a Christian in the sectarian sense, the example of Jesus' suffering is a factor in the composition of my underlying faith in nonviolence which rules all my actions, worldly and temporal. And I know that there are hundreds of Christians who believe likewise. Jesus lived and died in vain if he did not teach us to regulate the whole of life by the eternal Law of Love.

Gandhi and Jesus and Nonviolent Love

Terrence J. Rynne

Studying Gandhi's writings and reflecting on his life's work have changed the way I understand Jesus. When I read the New Testament I am thrilled and emboldened by the filled-with-compassion, brave, nonviolent Jesus I find there. Gandhi not only had a similar appreciation of Jesus but in his own life convincingly showed us that there is a way to live in this world actively working for the poor, taking on power structures and enduring violence without succumbing to violence oneself, his way of "satyagraha," which means "firmly holding to the truth" in the midst of conflict while reaching out with nonviolent, suffering love. When I read the Sermon on the Mount I hear Jesus proclaiming the same truth, the same "way": neither fight nor flight, but a third way of assertive, creative, nonviolent love even for our "enemies." When I see a crucifix I can only do what Gandhi did in the famous scene caught on film when he happened upon a simple crucifix while visiting the Vatican—bow and be grateful to Jesus for showing us the way and the power of suffering love.

I know I am not alone in finding inspiration from Gandhi to find in Jesus what the world, caught as it is in an iron spiral of violence, desperately needs. Andre Trocme, for example, the leader of the church in Chambon, France, that nonviolently resisted the Nazis and protected the lives of thousands of hunted Jewish people, wrote:

> The coming of Mahatma Gandhi, whose life and teaching surprisingly resemble those of Jesus, revived the whole issue of nonviolence just when majority theology thought it had already answered the question negatively. . . . Gandhi showed that the Sermon on the Mount can be politically effective.

Reading contemporary scripture scholarship has only confirmed for me this understanding of Jesus' life and teaching. There is great convergence of testimony from scripture scholars, that Jesus embodied and taught a way of nonviolent love of enemies and, in a time of violent Roman occupation of his country, gathered followers to live out that way. As one eminent scripture scholar, Norbert Lohfink, put it: "Jesus was nonviolent to the core."

Understanding Gandhian satyagraha has helped me understand and embrace Jesus' call to discipleship—following Jesus in his nonviolent Way of suffering, death, and resurrection. As a result, I understand what it means to be saved in a whole different way. It is to be united with him in the work of lifting up those whom society has left behind and in carrying on the work of building the Kingdom. This understanding has also given me a whole new understanding of the Mass. The Mass is not just an act of worship, an expression of a vertical relationship with God, nor is it only a meal that builds our horizontal relationships with our sisters and brothers. Even more important, in my life, the Mass is a summons to action, to live as Jesus did.

When I hear the words "Do this in memory of me," I am riveted. My back stiffens with resolve and my spirit and imagination are stirred. I think of the cloud of witnesses past and present who have modeled how to follow the nonviolent way, resisting oppression, caring for the poor and the sick, the outcast and the imprisoned, reaching out to "the enemy," confident in the love that possesses them. I think also of Gandhi's contention that it really is *ahimsa* that holds the world together, that violence is the rupture of the normal fabric of life—parents caring selflessly for their children, teachers engaging their students, people helping other people—that the daily round of human caring is what is real, not the *maya* of violence. Nonviolent action is the norm, not the exception.

I think also of how badly the world needs this message and this witness—how enmeshed our culture is in the belief in violence, how national security and the "nation" now command our deepest loyalty, how at risk we are because of our false idols.

The "this" in "Do this in memory of me" for me now means: "Do this way of acting that I have shown you. Do this way of resisting evil and returning good for evil that I lived and taught. Do it even if it is hard and stirs up resistance. Do it filled with love, because you know that you are loved." The Eucharist is now, for me, the call to follow Jesus' Way, united with him in his sacrifice and supported by a community of believers. It is the bread of life—sustenance for the journey, the Way that leads us outward and forward toward the suffering world.

Honoring George Floyd on 38th & Chicago

Greg Darr

As I made my way home after dark in a West Philadelphia neighborhood late in April 1992, I was set upon by a small group of youths carrying bats and boards. Hours earlier, a largely white jury had acquitted Los Angeles police officers of the brutal beating, captured on video, of Rodney King, an African-American man detained after a high-speed car chase. Los Angeles exploded into riot and arson. Across the country, Philadelphia hunkered down in fear. Even the homeless men with whom I worked as a Mercy Volunteer Corps volunteer were unusually subdued.

As I walked the final blocks home that evening, the group of youths caught sight of me. They laughed and jostled each other as they crossed the street to trap me. I had no time to think or even experience much fear before one of them struck me over the head and shoulders with a board. As I fell to the pavement, he leaned over and said,

"Tonight, we're white and you get to be black." And, with that, it was over. He leaned back up and, together with his friends, ambled away in laughter, leaving me sprawled alone on the sidewalk.

As I lay in shock, I soon felt an arm reach down and hook itself under mine. It belonged to one of the youths. He didn't say anything. He didn't even look at me. He just lifted me up and, when I was steady, let go and walked away just as silently to rejoin his friends.

After arriving home, I leaned back in safety on the closed door and started laughing and sobbing in the same halting breaths—laughing from relief that I returned intact and largely unhurt, and sobbing for reasons I still don't quite understand to this day.

This memory returned to me on the corner of 38th and Chicago a few days after George Floyd, an African-American man, had been tortuously killed there by Minneapolis police officers. My family and I had come to lay flowers at an improvised but rapidly growing memorial for him and other victims of police brutality. A few blocks to the north, a commercial neighborhood that I know well, lay in smoldering ruins. Later that night, the riots and fires would return.

At 38th and Chicago, however, my family and I experienced a surprising sense of peace. People of all colors and all walks of life—many of them together as families—came to share their grief, their stories, their fears and their hopes. In a frightened and besieged city, this intersection emerged as a singular place of personal and spiritual refuge.

It wasn't long before my wife and our two high-school-age daughters were enlisted by strangers to help paint banners, signage alerting arriving protesters or police of what we and many others already sensed: this was sacred space. In the meantime, organizers broke open boxes and distributed masks to those in need of COVID-19 protection. People did their best to maintain social distancing but, with that crowd size, it was nearly impossible.

As I listened to speaker after speaker relate experiences of police brutality and racism, protests and prayers intermingled to the point where they were no longer distinct. "How long, O Lord? Will you forget me forever. . . . Having sorrow in my heart all the day?" (Psalm 13) Psalmists and prophets would be "homies" in this crowd, their inspiration, if not their words, rendered now in hip-hop cadence.

It wasn't hard for me, a white man standing there, to recognize that there's not much systemically stacked against me. Even as a Maryknoll missionary in East Africa, I lived and worked in a bubble of racial privilege conferred upon me at birth. I can't change my skin color. But I can broaden my awareness and do my part, in solidarity with others, to lift unjust burdens that people of color carry on my behalf. It won't be easy, certainly for me. It's going to take patience, perseverance and, most of all, grace.

As I watched the bouquets, signs and written condolences pile higher in memory of George Floyd, I felt that grace move my heart. It was then I recalled that long-ago Philadelphia night and remembered, with gratitude, the youths who ambushed me and then helped me to my feet again. I gave thanks for the lessons they taught me. In a moment of violence and then compassion, they mocked my privileged innocence to a point where I could see it. They lifted me out of my lethargy and indifference in matters of race. And, they helped me to understand how racism stunts the emotional, mental, physical and spiritual health of everyone touched by it, including those privileged enough to believe it's not their problem. Most of all, considering the violence and poverty these youths faced daily, I experienced an extraordinary degree of mercy from them. I walked home a few bruises wiser and my wallet still in my pocket. These young men, on the other hand, walked from the scene down a far harder road. I wondered where it had taken them. Or, for someone like George Floyd, how far.

As I asked myself these questions, I watched a young man walk solemnly up to a mural painted in memory of George Floyd and other victims of police violence. He knelt, made the Sign of the Cross and prayed for a few moments. He again made the Sign of the Cross as he stood up and walked quietly away. Nearby, a little girl apparently took note of the young man's prayer. She stepped from her caregivers, returned to the mural where I had seen her wandering earlier, and knelt alone in her own sacred way of stillness.

Abraham Joshua Heschel, the Jewish scholar who, in 1965, participated in the Selma march with Dr. Martin Luther King Jr., observed, "Prayer is meaningless unless it is subversive, unless it seeks to overthrow and to ruin the pyramids of callousness, hatred, opportunism, falsehoods."

Prayer brings us to our knees. But, in matters of racism, justice and peace, it also hooks its arm under ours, lifts us up and sets us walking together on that hard uncertain road ahead. I stepped anew from the corner of 38th and Chicago, in memory of George Floyd and countless others, resolved to continue, with my brothers and sisters of color, on our way to the Promised Land.

❦

It's Up to All of Us

Michelle Obama

Race and racism is a reality that so many of us grow up learning to just deal with. But if we ever hope to move past it, it can't just be on people of color to deal with it. It's up to all of us—black, white, everyone—no matter how well-meaning we think we might be, to do the honest, uncomfortable work of rooting it out. It starts with self-examination and listening to those whose lives are different from our own. It ends with justice, compassion, and empathy that manifests in our lives and on our streets.

Bullets Don't Have No Names

Rivera Sun

On August 20, 2013, Antoinette Tuff nonviolently disarmed a school shooter, saving the lives of hundreds of school children. Antoinette was a bookkeeper. She wasn't supposed to be at the school that day. She was just filling in at the front office as a favor to a friend. That morning during her prayer time, she had read the Biblical passage, "Yea, though I walk through the valley of the shadow of death, I shall fear no evil." Little did she know that just a few hours later, twenty-year old Michael Brandon Hill would walk into the elementary school grounds in Dekalb County, Georgia, carrying an assault rifle and five hundred rounds of ammunition.

The police had arrived, the school was on lockdown, A toinette Tuff was alone in this part of the building. Mir Hill entered the room. Scared to the core, she obe⁾ initial commands, but then, for some reason, she ask I go to the bathroom?"

Those who have taken unarmed peacekeeping, peace team or de-escalation training will recognize this phenomenon at once: she broke the script, changed the narrative, and distracted Michael Hill from continuing on the track of senseless rage and disconnect that frequently occurs with mass shooters. In an interview reflecting on Antoinette Tuff's intervention, Kris Wilder, a 30-year veteran of the martial arts and author of *How To Win a Fight: A Guide to Avoiding and Surviving Violence,* is quoted as saying that one way to stop a dangerous situation is to change the channel with an out-of-the-blue question like "What time is it?" Or a nonsensical question like "What was Gandhi's batting average?"

To Antoinette Tuff's surprise, it worked. Michael Hill agreed to let her go to the bathroom. She rose to leave, but realized that the shooter might follow her to where the children were hiding. She hesitated. Then the situation worsened. Hill popped open the front door of the school and began firing at the police outside.

Antoinette Tuff sprang into action. Gently, lovingly, with a strange sense of calm, she said "Sweetheart, come back in here. Bullets don't have no names. And those bullets gonna kill me and you. I need you to come back in here, and it's gonna be me and you, and we will work this thing out."

Michael Hill retreated from the door, and Antoinette Tuff continued to talk, telling him about her marital troubles and how she had contemplated suicide several times. As she spoke, she found herself meeting his eyes and connecting to him as a human being. To her amazement,

Michael Hill began expressing his concerns and fears. Eventually, through dialogue and listening, empathizing and connecting, she convinced him to lay down his gun, and surrender to the police.

Antoinette's jaw-dropping story is an outstanding example of engaged nonviolence in the height of a violent situation. In speaking about her actions, Antoinette Tuff mentioned that she is a deeply spiritual person. She prayed for at least fifteen minutes each day and connected with her spiritual practice each night. Regardless of whether you are a Christian, Buddhist, Muslim, Hindu, Jewish, or some other faith, the practice of calming and centering the mind, grasping your inner strength, seeing with compassion, and rooting yourself in faith is an invaluable preparation for engaging active nonviolence in the world.

Pause for Peace

The half of humanity that have never bourne arms is today ready to struggle to make the brotherhood of man a reality. Perhaps the universal sisterhood is necessary before the universal brotherhood is possible.

—Bertha von Suttner

We cannot all succeed when half of us are held back.

—Malala Yousafzai

Girls everywhere are strong, they are capable and they will determine our future.

—Angelica Fuentes

Pause for Peace

Women are symbols of love. Mothers embody love and compassion. Sometimes I observe that if countries had more women leaders, we'd have a more peaceful world.

—DALAI LAMA

We are all meant to be mothers of God.

—MEISTER ECKHART

Ain't I a Woman?

Sojourner Truth

Then that little man in black there, he says women can't have as much rights as men, 'cause Christ wasn't a woman! Where did your Christ come from? Where did your Christ come from? From God and a woman! Man had nothing to do with Him. If the first woman God ever made was strong enough to turn the world upside down all alone, these women together ought to be able to turn it back and get it right side up again! And now they is asking to do it, the men better let them. Obliged to you for hearing me, and now old Sojourner ain't got nothing more to say.

Love Is the Answer

Dorothy Day

Deliver us, Lord, from the fear of the enemy. That is one of the lines in the Psalms, and we are not asking God to deliver us from enemies but from the fear of them. Love casts out fear, but we have to get over the fear in order to get close enough to love them.

There is plenty to do, for each one of us, working on our own hearts, changing our own attitudes, in our own neighborhoods. If the just man falls seven times daily, we each one of us fall more than that in thought, word, and deed. Prayer and fasting, taking up our own cross daily and following Him, doing penance, these are the hard words of the Gospel. As to the Church, where else shall we go, except to the Bride of Christ, one flesh with Christ? Though she is a harlot at times, she is our Mother. We should read the Book of Hosea, which is a picture of God's steadfast love not only for the Jews, His chosen people, but for His Church, of which we are every one of us members or potential members. Since there is no time with God, we are all one, all one body, Chinese, Russians, Vietnamese and He has *commanded us to love one another.*

"A new commandment I give, that you love others *as I have loved you*," not to the defending of your life, but to the laying down of your life.

A hard saying.

Love is indeed a "harsh and dreadful thing" to ask of us, of each one of us, but it is the only answer.

Dorothy Day came on a quite simple,
paradoxical insight, something like this:
in the Gospel, peace is a verb. You make
the peace. You do not inherit it, or hoard
it, or borrow it, or sit on it. You make it.
—DANIEL BERRIGAN

31

My Enemy Has Become My Friend

Joan Chittister

It was a hot and honest session in that meeting of Palestinian and Israeli women in Oslo, Norway. The Palestinian women said that they supported the Israelis' right to an independent state; the Israeli women said that they supported the Palestinians' right to resources, political integrity, and freedom to live in the land. It was a significant political moment.

Nevertheless, what happened after the conference adjourned may, in the end, prove to be even more significant.

On the last night of the assembly, one of these women went to the other and asked to continue the discussion about what had been lost and what must be gained if the two peoples are ever to live together well. They went out for coffee together. I don't know what was said. I only know that the conversation went on until after midnight.

When it came time to leave, the Israeli woman—old enough to be the Palestinian's mother—decided she would walk the young woman to her hotel. But then the young Palestinian realized how far the older woman would have to walk alone back to her own place of residence and insisted that she walk her halfway back again.

"I've had a wonderful night," the Israeli woman said as they parted. "This time with you was itself worth the conference." The young Palestinian woman went silent for a moment. "I'm glad for you," she said, "but I'm confused."

The Israeli woman winced inside, "Why? What's wrong?" she asked.

"Oh, nothing is wrong," the younger woman said. "I'm just confused. I don't know what to do now that my enemy has become my friend."

The next day, in the Tel Aviv airport, the Israeli women whisked through customs and baggage claim. The Palestinian women did not. When the Israeli women realized that all the Palestinians had been detained, they turned around, went back and refused to leave the customs hall themselves until all the Palestinians were released.

That, I learned, is what it means to proceed in the "ways of peace." It means having the courage to make human connections with those we fear, with those we hate, with those who think differently than we do. It means refusing to leave the other behind as we go.

32

Abigail the Peacemaker

Susanne Guenther Loewen

This week I was reminded of a biblical figure who is often overlooked: Abigail (or, as my Bible disappointingly calls her, "the wife of Nabal"!). Her story is found in I Samuel 25. I find it intriguing as a woman and as a Mennonite pacifist, because Abigail is, arguably and perhaps unexpectedly, a master peacemaker, someone who prevents a lot of needless bloodshed through her wise and well-timed words and actions.

To summarize her story briefly: Abigail, a woman described as "clever and beautiful," is married to Nabal, a man who is reportedly "surly and mean." David, who is not yet king, is travelling through Nabal's territory with a small army, and he sends a message to Nabal. It begins, "Peace be to you, and peace be to your house, and peace be to all that you have." David continues by asking that since he and his army have not hurt Nabal's shepherds or sheep while travelling through, and in fact protected them, could Nabal provide them with a feast? In other words, having acted honourably toward and protected Nabal's property and servants, David and his men ask for his hospitality in return. But Nabal refuses to provide a feast for them, since they are strangers and nobodies as far as he's concerned.

Upon hearing this message, David is furious, and issues his orders: "Every man strap on his sword!" And his 400-person army obeys.

But Abigail hears about her husband's insulting behaviour towards David, the way he returned "evil for good," and she acts quickly to right the situation. She gathers a feast's-worth of food, loads it onto donkeys, and rides out herself on a donkey to meet David and his soldiers. She apologizes profusely, asks for David's forgiveness, takes responsibility for the misunderstanding, reminds David that Nabal lives up to his name (which means "folly"!). She assures David that she did not see the messengers he sent—otherwise, the response would have been much different! She speaks self-deprecatingly (calling herself a servant and David "lord" and the future "prince over Israel"), but she also, interestingly, makes her case *theologically*, telling David that *God* "has restrained you from bloodguilt and from taking vengeance with your own hand" and that *God* will bless him in the future because he "shall have no cause of grief, or pangs of conscience, for having shed blood without cause or for having saved himself" (vv. 26, 30–31).

And Abigail's ingenious speech about how it would be against God's will for David to carry out his plan of violently attacking Nabal's household is so masterfully argued that he's immediately and wholeheartedly convinced! He even speaks of Abigail as God's own emissary.

"Blessed be the Lord, the God of Israel, who sent you to meet me today!" David says to Abigail. "Blessed be your good sense, and blessed be you, who have kept me today from bloodguilt and from avenging myself by my own hand! For as surely as the Lord the God of Israel lives, who has restrained me from hurting you, unless you had hurried and come to meet me, truly by morning there would not have been left to Nabal so much as one male" (vv. 32–34).

So instead of slaughtering Abigail and her whole household, David and his army share the feast that she provides for them. David's farewell words to her are: "Go up to your house in peace; see, I have heeded your voice, and I have granted your petition."

Abigail returns to her house and eventually tells her husband about how she made peace with David and prevented his army from unleashing violence upon them. Nabal is so shocked that "his heart died within him; he became like a stone." He dies ten days later, leaving Abigail free, in a strange twist, to become David's wife—or rather, one of David's wives. She clearly made quite an impression on him!

I appreciate how this story bends or even subverts our expectations on a few different levels. For one thing, it's a story about a non-Israelite teaching David a lesson about a theology of peace. The story just preceding it is about how David has a chance to kill Saul (then the king of Israel, whom David will succeed) but decides not to, and Saul's expression of gratitude. He says to David: "You are more righteous than I; for you have repaid me good, whereas I have repaid you evil" (I Sam. 24:17).

Just after this act of mercy on David's part, he is about to turn to violence again because now Nabal has returned "evil for good," but Abigail, through quick thinking, an articulate speech, sound theologizing (she clearly knows about Israelite notions of bloodguilt), and a generous act of hospitality, reminds David to again exercise mercy. Not only that, she reminds him that God wants him to repay evil with good instead of further evil, to act with mercy instead of violence or vengeance—a message which must have turned David's own expectations about these non-Israelites on their heads.

It's also notable that Abigail is a woman. Though there are ways in which she falls into more traditional/patriarchal gender expectations, especially in her almost annoyingly self-deprecating servant-language for herself and overly-elevated language for David in her speech to him—not to mention her later agreement to become part of his harem of wives!

But in other ways, she's a wise, courageous, and defiant peacemaker—even David praises her "good sense." She takes initiative (and defies her husband) to prevent the disaster which her husband's foolishness (i.e., macho posturing) has brought on their entire household, and she takes the considerable risk of meeting David and his army of 400 in person (which her husband never did) to speak convincingly about peace and to offer a delicious feast (of bread, wine, mutton, raisins, and figs!).

Armed only with words and food, Abigail faces an army! What a beautiful example of the love of enemies in action! In this way, amazingly, she makes peace and she ends up feasting with David and his army instead of becoming a helpless and tragic victim of their violence.

Finally, this story subverts our smug Christian assumptions that the Hebrew Scriptures (Old Testament) are saturated with violence, while the New Testament contains a brand-new, unprecedented message of peace. These assumptions far too easily slip into Christian supersessionism (the belief that Christians replaced Jews as the chosen people of God).

Honestly, how many of us would think of the combination of "Old Testament" and "peace" as a bit of an oxymoron? But in this story, as in others in the Hebrew Scriptures, we catch a glimpse of a thread of pacifism, nonviolence, or peace theology that is unquestionably rooted in the Jewish tradition (and thus runs throughout the entire Bible, not just the New Testament).

In this way, we can think of Abigail as a forbear in faith—a fellow peacemaker in the tradition of Jewish pacifism—to Someone in the later lineage of David who also rode on a donkey, feasted instead of fighting, spoke eloquently of peace, and (admittedly, much more famously) advocated the love of enemies.

Pause for Peace

*Peace is not something you wish for, it's
something you make. Something you
do. Something you are, and something
you give away.*

—JOHN LENNON

*When the power of love overcomes
the love of power the world will know
peace.*

—JIMI HENDRIX

*If you don't know the guy on the other
side of the world, love him anyway
because he's just like you. He has the
same dreams, the same hopes and fears.
It's one world, pal. We're all neighbors.*

—FRANK SINATRA

Pause for Peace

I believe in peace and love and unity.
I believe that this vision can be a reality.
And, it's not about me. It's about WE.
Together we can give birth to a kinder
and more peaceful world for ALL
children.
Our souls were brought together so that
we can love each other sister, brother.
We are here. We are here for all of us.

—ALICIA KEYES

That's all nonviolence is—organized
love.

—JOAN BAEZ

33

Construct No Walls around "Sacred Space"

Francine Dempsey

Images of endless war, overflowing refugee camps, hate-filled terrorists, billion-dollar weapons, starved children—I want to flee this world's violence. So I ask my prayer group, women who, like me, have lived through many decades totally safe from such horrible experiences: "What am I to do?"

Pat, 85, says, "I'm reading the letters of Etty Hillesum." I recall from a long-ago reading of *An Interrupted Life* that Etty died in a concentration camp during the Holocaust.

Pat explains that while imprisoned by German invaders in Westerbork, a concentration camp near her Netherlands home, Etty wrote numerous letters to family and friends. While each day she watched as guards packed a train's boxcars with human cargo bound for Auschwitz and death—simply for being Jews—she wrote letters filled with stories of men and women doing good.

Later, I find a library copy of Etty's book.

Throughout, Etty describes the human suffering but also the human goodness that happens day after day, week after week, month after month, as the trains come, again and again. I ponder Etty's words: "Despite everything, life is full of beauty and meaning." And, "We have been marked by suffering for a whole lifetime. And yet life in its unfathomable depths is so wonderfully good."

One day it is Etty's turn to board her boxcar on the train that also carries her parents to Auschwitz. In her final written words, discovered on a postcard she throws from the moving train, Etty, a woman of deep spirituality, quotes Scripture: "The Lord is my high tower." Of herself and her mother and father, weakened and ill after their Westerbork life of near starvation, exposure to extreme heat, cold, overcrowded rooms and mattress-less bunks, Etty proclaims: "We left the camp singing."

I ask myself, can Westerbork, a place of unimaginable human suffering, be a "sacred place" or "holy ground," maybe even more so than the pure, placid, peaceful church or synagogue or mosque or temple space?

Can I image Syria or Afghanistan or Yemen or Sudan or Somalia or a refugee camp holding 180,000, places of war and famine, death and starvation, as places where human goodness endures, as sacred places "full of meaning and beauty," where angels and humans are singing a chorus of beauty in the midst of ugliness?

This is a struggle in two ways. First, I know belief in human goodness everywhere must not blind me to the horrors of violent war, raging famine. I must not be a Pollyanna, must never stop my efforts to end endless war, to assist refugees and victims of famine, to resist injustice, including my own, in its many forms.

Yet I must at the same time know that I am walking in a sacred space with truly holy men and women in war zones and refugee camps, doing endless acts of human kindness, of love, amid their suffering, even their suffering unto death.

Second, like Etty, I must face my willingness to construct walls around my comforting image of "sacred space," my letting into the sacred space only the imprisoned, the suffering, while excluding the "other," the perpetrators of the violence—the enemy. Etty struggles with God's command to love all in a much more difficult situational barrier to oneness. But she refuses to let hate into her heart. Of the guards she says, "I have never been so frightened of anything in my life. I sank to my knees with the words that preside over human life: 'And God made man after His likeness.' That passage spent a difficult morning with me."

So in my born-a-Catholic heart I must struggle with "Love your enemies." "They know not what they do." "I have come to save sinners." In God, there is only one sacred space.

Like most 21st-century religious pushing 80, I am called by the new creation story, new science, new theology. I am learning of the "oneness" that in recent years scientists and theologians pose as the heart of reality.

Since 2000, my religious community has called me to prayer that seeks oneness, communion: centering prayer, contemplative prayer, even mystical prayer. In this world so fractured, so full of noise, religious community members, like so many others, are seeking to find that deep silence, deep prayer, deep connection with God, so essential to knowing our oneness with God and all that is in God and bringing that oneness to all.

So with Etty's help I reconstruct my image of sacred space. Can I in my heart hold all as sacred? Each night in my prayer, I wrap God's encircling, unconditional love around the suffering and the inflictors of the suffering, and yes, they are one with me.

> *Ultimately, we have just one moral duty: to reclaim large areas of peace in ourselves, more and more peace, and to reflect it towards others. And the more peace there is in us, the more peace there will also be in our troubled world.*
>
> —ETTY HILLESUM

34

Peace Pilgrim

Robert Ellsberg

*I am a pilgrim, a wanderer. I shall
remain a wanderer until mankind has
learned the way of peace, walking until
I am given shelter and fasting until I
am given food.*

She called herself Peace Pilgrim. Otherwise she had no
interest in describing the particulars of her early life, her
age, or even her given name. She walked back and forth
across the United States for almost three decades, owning
nothing but the clothes she wore: a pair of navy blue slacks
and a blue shirt, blue sneakers, and a tunic bearing her
chosen name and, on the back in white letters, the simple
words, "25,000 Miles on Foot for Peace."

As far as she would reveal, Pilgrim's early years were
conventional and uneventful. Like other people she had
pursued money and possessions. But at a certain point

she realized that this "self-centered" existence did not bring fulfillment. After spending one night wandering in the woods she came to "a complete willingness, without any reservations, to give my life to God and to service." "Please use me!" she prayed to God. "And a great peace came over me."

So began a long, fifteen-year period of preparation for an as-yet undefined mission. Embracing a life of simplicity, she worked as a volunteer with various social service and peace organizations. Apart from weaning herself from material possessions, she also pursued an arduous course of spiritual discipline to adjust to the demands of a "God-centered existence." She was determined to live by what she called "the laws that govern the universe." These included the fact that evil can be overcome only by good; that only good means can attain a good end; that those who do unloving things hurt themselves spiritually.

Among the disciplines she practiced were purification of the body, purification of thought ("I don't eat junk foods and I don't think junk thoughts"), and purification of desire and motive (doing nothing for self-glory or other impure ends). She also practiced various "relinquishments," letting go of the feeling of "separateness," of attachments, and of all negative feelings.

There came a point one morning when she suddenly felt uplifted in a dimension of "timelessness, spacelessness, and lightness." She seemed not to be walking on the earth. "Every flower, every bush, every tree seemed to wear a halo. There was a light emanation around everything, and flecks of gold fell like slanted rain through the air." During this time of illumination she conceived her life mission: she would go on pilgrimage for peace, praying constantly, rousing people from their apathy and awakening the hearts of all whom she encountered.

Pilgrim set off from Los Angeles on January 1, 1953. The war in Korea was raging. Nuclear arsenals were proliferating around the globe. The McCarthy-era investigations were smelling treason in every corner, raising suspicions that even the word "Peace" was simply a shrewd disguise for subversion.

Peace Pilgrim set off with no publicity and no organizational backing. Carrying nothing but what she could hold in the pockets of her tunic—a toothbrush, a pen, and leaflets to distribute to anyone who asked—she simply walked from town to town, and eventually state to state. She accepted food and hospitality when it was offered. Otherwise she fasted or slept outdoors—under a tree or a bridge, or simply in the nearest field. The bold words on her tunic proclaimed her message and invited conversation with curious passersby. To whomever she met she described her purpose: "My pilgrimage covers the entire peace picture: peace among nations, peace among groups, peace within our environment, peace among individuals, and the very, very important inner peace."

Newspapers and eventually television journalists publicized her travels. She was invited to speak in countless schools, churches, and universities. Sometimes she was arrested as a vagrant. She considered such adventures no distraction from her essential mission. Wherever she went she engaged her listeners as human beings, bearers of the image of God, with whom she eagerly shared her teachings: how to overcome evil with good, falsehood with truth, hatred with love.

By 1964 her pilgrimage had surpassed her original goal of twenty-five thousand miles. After that she ceased counting. But she did not cease walking. Long after her hair had turned silver with age, she maintained her constant pilgrimage, showing no loss of energy or enthusiasm with the passing years. It was not the walking that killed her. She made what she liked to call "the glorious transition to a freer life" on July 7, 1981, when a car in which she was being driven to a speaking engagement was hit in a head-on collision.

"Who am I?" she had written. "It matters not that you know who I am, it is of little importance. This clay garment is one of a penniless pilgrim journeying in the name of peace. It is what you cannot see that is so very important. I am one who is propelled by the power of faith; I bathe in the light of eternal wisdom; I am sustained by the unending energy of the universe; this is who I really am."

What We Dwell Upon Happens

Peace Pilgrim

A few really dedicated people can offset the masses of out of harmony people, so we who work for peace must not falter, we must continue to pray for peace and to act for peace in whatever way we can. We must continue to speak for peace and to live the way of peace; to inspire others, we must continue to think of peace and know that peace is possible. What we dwell upon we help bring to manifestation. One little person giving all of her time to peace makes news. Many people giving some of their time can make history.

Daring to Be Human

Magda Yoors-Peeters

I am a Belgian woman. During the Great War I hated the Germans with the bitterest hatred. I wanted the French and the Belgians to fight more and to crush Germany. So I preached hate. I not only talked it, but I wrote it. I wrote articles for the magazines and the papers to create more hatred of the Germans. And I succeeded. People listened and read what I wrote. Then they too would hate more deeply and more bitterly than before.

It was one winter in the war time that I was in Holland with my husband. We were doing relief work there among the Belgian refugees. We rented a room from a Dutch family, and the man and woman felt as we did about the Germans. They also hated, as we hated. We had many Belgian refugees to care for, and we were very busy.

This story was told by Magda Yoors-Peeters at the conference of the International Fellowship of Reconciliation at Nyborg Strand, Denmark, in 1923.

One day my husband and I were walking along a road near the town, not many miles from the border of Germany. We saw ahead of us something lying in the mud, and when we came nearer we saw it was a man. We stooped over him and saw he was in the uniform of a German soldier. He was a German. His shoes were broken, so his feet showed through, and his feet were all muddy and bleeding.

We looked at him. We could not leave him lying there in the cold. What could we do? We could not take him to the house of the Dutch people, because they hated the Germans just as we did. But he needed help; he was faint with hunger and cold. He did not even know he was in Holland and not in Germany. We stood looking down at him.

Then suddenly we decided to take him to the house and try to get him in without the knowledge of the landlady. We helped him, between us, back to the town and into the house. The landlady fortunately was not around. We put him on the bed in our room.

What could we do? His feet were bloody and dirty. I had to wash them! So I got some water and a cloth and knelt down to wash his feet. While I was washing his feet something happened inside me. Something fell down from my eyes, and I saw that he was a brother. A German was my brother. The Germans were our brothers.

Then we had to get him something to eat, he was so hungry. It was war time, of course, and we had only one egg apiece every two weeks. But I went downstairs and asked the landlady for two eggs!

"Two eggs," she exclaimed, "and what would you be doing with two eggs at once in war time?" I had to tell her the truth. There was a German soldier upstairs; his feet were bleeding; he was hungry and faint and cold. Yes, he was a German, but—

The landlady looked at me a moment. Her eyes filled with tears, and then she said, "Take the two eggs. And here's some jam I made; take that up to him. But don't you tell my husband!"

When he had eaten and was warm, my husband and I put on him some of the clothes we had ready for the Belgian refugees—a new pair of shoes and a suit of clothes.

It was late in the afternoon and almost dark. He started out from the house to find his way back to the German border. We stood at the window and watched him go. The snowflakes began to come down, slowly and steadily, then faster and faster. He would be wet through in the storm. Would he get back to the border? Would he be safe? We never knew. We never heard of him again.

Pause for Peace

My first wish is to see this plague of mankind, war, banished from the earth.
—George Washington

As the War Office of the United States was established in a time of peace, it is equally reasonable that a Peace Office should be established in a time of War.
—Benjamin Rush

Join me in support for building a U.S. Department of Peace to address issues of peace-building here at home—trauma-informed education, community wrap-around services, restorative justice, conflict resolution, mindfulness in the schools, violence prevention programs, and more.

—Marianne Williamson

Pause for Peace

I like to believe that people in the long run are going to do more to promote peace than are governments. Indeed, I think that people want peace so much that one of these days governments had better get out of their way and let them have it.

—Dwight D. Eisenhower

"Peace, Peace."
But for Whom?

Cindy Brandt

When I was living in China, taxis were a convenient and cheap mode of transportation. One time, our taxi driver got into a small fender bender. The cabbie of the offended party got out of his car and began walking towards us shouting angry retorts, garbled in the thick Tianjin accent I was yet getting used to, laced with a few profanities. In a few strides he came to reach past the rolled down window of our driver and landed a punch. An all-out fistfight was brewing while in the backseat my toddler blew spit bubbles at me.

When I tell my China stories, they come out sounding outlandish without me embellishing with details. The reality is, it was quite a part of our ordinary lives to witness fist fights in China. Taxi drivers wore their road rage on the outside, shoving when necessary, hitting when riled up. It happened all the time.

In my initial stages of culture shock, I was extremely uncomfortable and frightened when physical violence broke out like that, but I soon realized that nobody ever ends up being (very) hurt. Thirteen million people lived in our city so every fight was a public spectacle. Before long, a mob of people would descend upon the two men engaged in a fistfight and forcibly break them up. The ladies get in there too, which I love.

"*Suan le ba, suan le ba,*" they would say. "Just forget it, let it go."

At this point, the men being dragged away from each other would punch a few more times into the air at the other guy, just for show, and go back to regular programming.

The act of breaking up fistfights was physical and volatile, and it was always done by a group of people. Not necessarily because the strength of the fighting men required it, but more as a signal of group solidarity. We want you to stop fighting.

Peace, with its connotation of tranquility and stillness, is the Christian's most misunderstood concept. We have long sought to keep peace by silencing dissent under the guise of pursuing unity, coated with a zealous concern for niceties, unwilling to budge a status quo. We forget to ask the crucial question: for whom do we keep peace?

Wherever peace is elusive, the first ones to suffer are the vulnerable.

When corporations engage in legal battles, employees who don't get a vote have the most at stake. When marital tensions rise high, children's tender spirits lay at the parents' mercy. When war ravages a country, the displaced peoples helplessly suffer.

When keeping the peace only benefits the powerful, it is not a Christian peace. The sweet baby Jesus portrayed in sentimental Christmas cards has taken an abrupt departure from the kind of peace we see Jesus embody in Scripture. Even as an infant, the baby Jesus so disrupted the power authorities of the day that sent them scrambling into every home killing firstborn baby boys.

The same Jesus grew to preach radical teachings such as: the first shall be last, love your enemies, grace and mercy shall transcend the law. This Prince of Peace turned tables in a marketplace of greed, shared meals with unclean people, and wept with grieving women. This King marched into Jerusalem on a donkey, was tried by the reigning religious authority of the day, and was executed as a political dissident. His peace did not protect the powerful—it disrupted the systems, brazenly paving a new way and inviting those in the margins to follow.

Christian peace is not about coddling people's fear of conflict. It isn't about making sure everyone is comfortable. It does not silence those for whom a lack of peace is a life or death situation. The irony is that often, the ones with feeble power are the ones who are told to keep peace and remain silent.

When the society is disrupted by scandalizing conflict— whether it is the Bill Cosby rape accusations, or the "harsh disciplinary methods" of certain celebrity parents, or an entire neighborhood weary of losing their young men to police violence—the Christian dare not keep peace by silencing the voice of the victims. Instead, we must make room for the disruptions to take place, to let the voices of those marginalized wear down the reigning power structures. The Christian should not accuse the cries of minorities as "oversensitive," the desperate pleas of abuse victims as "unforgiving," and the repetitive calls for gender equality as "whiny," or "shrill."

If the scandal disturbs us, upsets us, makes us uncomfortable, then we may congratulate ourselves for being on the right track to peacemaking, because that is also where Jesus began.

The reigning Roman Empire of Jesus' day appeared peaceful. Merchants were flourishing, the economy was booming, the religious structures intact to maintain order and complicity from her citizens. Yet behind that veneer of civilization was a superficial peace extracted from violence, a society built on the backs of slave labor and spiritual oppression of legalism.

The cross pierced that veneer, exposing a false peace to make way for lasting peace. Jesus took real action for peace, even when it cost his life. As followers of Jesus, let's shed the passivity of peace-keeping in exchange for active engagement of peace-making. Like the mobs on the Chinese streets, let's not walk past the disruptions of peace by turning a blind eye, but involve ourselves with our hands and feet.

In solidarity we proclaim: we demand true peace.

38

Planting Seeds

Megan McKenna

There was a woman who wanted peace in the world and peace in her heart and all sorts of good things, but she was very frustrated. The world seemed to be falling apart. She would read the papers and get depressed. One day she decided to go shopping, and she went into a mall and picked a store at random. She walked in and was surprised to see Jesus behind the counter. She knew it was Jesus, because he looked just like the pictures she'd seen on holy cards and devotional pictures. She looked again and again at him, and finally she got up her nerve and asked, "Excuse me, are you Jesus?" "I am." "Do you work here?" "No," Jesus said, "I own the store." "Oh, what do you sell in here?" "Oh, just about anything!" "Anything?" "Yeah, anything you want. What do you want?" She said, "I don't know." "Well," Jesus said, "feel free, walk up and down the aisles, make a list, see what it is you want, and then come back and we'll see what we can do for you."

She did just that, walked up and down the aisles. There was peace on earth, no more war, no hunger or poverty, peace in families, no more drugs, harmony, clean air, careful use of resources. She wrote furiously. By the time she got back to the counter, she had a long list. Jesus took the list, skimmed through it, looked up at her and smiled. "No problem." And then he bent down behind the counter and picked out all sorts of things, stood up, and laid out the packets. She asked, "What are these?" Jesus replied, "Seed packets. This is a catalog store." She said, "You mean I don't get the finished product?" "No, this is a place of dreams. You come and see what it looks like, and I give you the seeds. You plant the seeds. You go home and nurture them and help them to grow and someone else reaps the benefits." "Oh," she said. And she left the store without buying anything.

If we don't get what we want right away, then maybe we don't really want it, or we don't want it enough. This is discouraging. We may have seen the dream of the kingdom. We may know exactly how the kingdom comes, but that doesn't mean that we bring it, or contribute to it, or are a part of it. We are all reaping the benefits of those who have gone before us in faith and life. But we need to stop and ask ourselves what we are doing for others. What seeds are we planting and nourishing? Our religion teaches that it is not primarily what we do for ourselves or our own, but what we do for others, for the outsiders, the strangers, that reveals our belief.

39

The Call of Conscience

Parker J. Palmer

I have another friend who has devoted most of his adult life to resisting the madness of war through actions of justice and peace. He has done everything from painfully unearthing the seeds of violence in his personal life to living in poverty so as to stay below the taxation level. He owns nothing in his own name because, if he did, the government could collect it as back-taxes. The money he "should" have given the government over the years, and more, he has donated to peace and justice projects.

Does he have any results to show for his efforts? Has he been effective? Hardly—at least, not by the normal calculus. His years of commitment to peacemaking have been years of steady increase in wars and rumors of wars. So how does he stay healthy and sane? How does he maintain a commitment to this sort of active life? His answer completes the koan offered by my friend at the Catholic Worker: "I have never asked myself if I was being effective, but only if I was being faithful." He judges his action, not by the results it gets, but by its fidelity to his own calling and identity.

40

What We Are Asked to Do

Martin Sheen

I have been an actor all my life. In fact, I have no conscious
memory of ever not being an actor. I couldn't identify it as
such when I was a child, until I started going to the mov-
ies around the age five or six, and then it gradually began
to dawn on me that, Oh, I was one of those people up on
the screen. And it was an extremely comforting revelation
because I knew even then, that I would never be happy
unless I pursued that wondrous mystery that possessed me,
and it gave me a possession of myself. So in a sense, my
chosen profession was a foregone conclusion, and taking
it all and all, I have not the slightest regret.

But while acting is what I do for a living, activism is what
I do to stay alive. And I'm often asked how I came to unite

Excerpted from Martin Sheen's acceptance speech for the Notre
Dame Laetare Medal Award, the most prestigious award for service
to church and humanity an American Catholic can receive, on May
17, 2008.

the two, and the answer is simple, I haven't a clue. But it was less a conscious effort than it was a natural progression. I learned early on that you serve yourself best when you serve others first. Of course, if you grow up in a large, poor, immigrant family, chances are you're either Irish-Catholic or Hispanic. I was lucky enough to be both, so I had a huge advantage when it came to social justice activism.

Indeed the truth is mighty and it shall prevail.

Each time someone stands up for an ideal, or acts to improve the lot of others, or strikes out against injustice, they send forth a tiny ripple of hope and crossing each other from a million different centers of energy and daring, those ripples build a current which can sweep down the mightiest walls of repression and injustice.

Those words were spoken at the University of Capetown in South Africa in 1966 by Robert Francis Kennedy. They are enshrined on his memorial at Arlington National Cemetery as well, and they have been a powerful source of inspiration for my generation ever since.

Whether we acknowledge it or not, we are all responsible for each other and the world, which is exactly the way it is, because consciously or unconsciously, we have made it so. And while none of us made any of the rules that govern the universe or the human heart, we are all beneficiaries of a divine promise, that the world is still a safe place despite our fears, and we in it are not asked to do great things; we are asked to do all things with great love.

Pause for Peace

Change will not come if we wait for some other person, or if we wait for some other time. We are the ones we've been waiting for. We are the change that we seek.

—BARACK OBAMA

I have one life and one chance to make it count for something. . . . My faith demands that I do whatever I can, wherever I am, whenever I can, for as long as I can, with whatever I have to try to make a difference.

—JIMMY CARTER

With a good conscience our only sure reward, with history the final judge of our deeds, let us go forth to lead the

*land we love, asking His blessing and
His help, but knowing that here on
earth God's work must truly be our
own.*

—JOHN F. KENNEDY

*International exchanges are not a great
tide to sweep away all differences, but
they will slowly wear away at the ob-
stacles to peace as surely as water wears
away a hard stone.*

—GEORGE H. W. BUSH

*To live together and work together.
That's how I see America. That's how
I see the presidency, and that's how I
see the future.*

—JOE BIDEN

Reach for the World That Ought to Be

Barack Obama

The one rule that lies at the heart of every major religion is that we do unto others as we would have them do unto us.

Adhering to this law of love has always been the core struggle of human nature. For we are fallible. We make mistakes, and fall victim to the temptations of pride, and power, and sometimes evil. Even those of us with the best of intentions will at times fail to right the wrongs before us.

But we do not have to think that human nature is perfect for us to still believe that the human condition can be perfected. We do not have to live in an idealized world to still reach for those ideals that will make it a better place. The nonviolence practiced by men like Gandhi and King may not have been practical or possible in every circumstance, but the love that they preached—their fundamental faith in human progress—that must always be the North Star that guides us on our journey.

For if we lose that faith—if we dismiss it as silly or naive; if we divorce it from the decisions that we make on issues of war and peace—then we lose what's best about humanity. We lose our sense of possibility. We lose our moral compass.

Like generations have before us, we must reject that future. As Dr. King said at this occasion so many years ago, "I refuse to accept despair as the final response to the ambiguities of history. I refuse to accept the idea that the 'isness' of man's present condition makes him morally incapable of reaching up for the eternal 'oughtness' that forever confronts him."

Let us reach for the world that ought to be—that spark of the divine that still stirs within each of our souls.

Somewhere today, in the here and now, in the world as it is, a soldier sees he's outgunned, but stands firm to keep the peace. Somewhere today, in this world, a young protestor awaits the brutality of her government, but has the courage to march on. Somewhere today, a mother facing punishing poverty still takes the time to teach her child, scrapes together what few coins she has to send that child to school—because she believes that a cruel world still has a place for that child's dreams.

Let us live by their example. We can acknowledge that oppression will always be with us, and still strive for justice. We can admit the intractability of depravation, and still strive for dignity. Clear-eyed, we can understand that there will be war, and still strive for peace. We can do that—for that is the story of human progress; that's the hope of all the world; and at this moment of challenge, that must be our work here on Earth.

42

No Man Is an Island

Thomas Merton

Violence rests on the assumption that the enemy and I are entirely different: the enemy is evil and I am good. The enemy must be destroyed but I must be saved. But love sees things differently. It sees that even the enemy suffers from the same sorrows and limitations that I do. That we both have the same hopes, the same needs, the same aspiration for a peaceful and harmless human life. And that death is the same for both of us. Then love may perhaps show me that my brother is not really my enemy and that war is both his enemy and mine. War is *our* enemy. Then peace becomes possible.

It is true, political problems are not solved by love and mercy. But the world of politics is not the only world, and unless political decisions rest on a foundation of something better and higher than politics, they can never do any real good for men. When a country has to be rebuilt after war, the passions and energies of war are no longer enough.

There must be a new force, the power of love, the power of understanding and human compassion, the strength of selflessness and cooperation, and the creative dynamism of *the will to live and to build, and the will to forgive. The will for reconciliation.*

We must all believe in love and in peace. We must believe in the power of love. We must recognize that our being itself is grounded in love; that is to say, that we come into being because we are loved and because we are meant to love others. The failure to believe this and to live accordingly creates instead a deep mistrust, a suspicion of others, a hatred of others, a failure to love. When a man attempts to live by and for himself alone, he becomes a little "island" of hate, greed, suspicion, fear, desire. Then his whole outlook on life is falsified. All his judgments are affected by that untruth. In order to recover the true perspective, which is that of love and compassion, he must once again learn, in simplicity, truth, and peace, that "No man is an island."

43

When Peace Becomes Obnoxious

Martin Luther King Jr.

A few weeks ago, a Federal Judge handed down an edict which stated in substance that the University of Alabama could no longer deny admission to persons because of their race. With the handing down of this decision, a brave young lady by the name of Autherine Lucy was accepted as the first Negro student to be admitted in the history of the University of Alabama. This was a great moment and a great decision. But with the announcement of this decision, "the vanguards of the old order began to surge." The forces of evil began to congeal. As soon as Autherine Lucy walked on the campus, a group of spoiled students led by Leonard Wilson and a vicious group of outsiders began threatening her on every hand. Crosses were burned; eggs and bricks were thrown at her. The mob jumped on top of the car in which she was riding. Finally, the president and trustees of the University of Alabama asked Autherine to leave for her own safety and the safety of the University. The next day after Autherine was dismissed, the paper came out with this headline: "Things are quiet in Tuscaloosa today. There is peace on the campus of the University of Alabama."

Yes, things are quiet in Tuscaloosa. Yes, there was peace on the campus, but it was peace at a great price: it was peace that had been purchased at the exorbitant price of an inept trustee board succumbing to the whims and caprices of a vicious mob. It was peace that had been purchased at the price of allowing mobocracy to reign supreme over democracy. It was peace that had been purchased at the price of capitulating to the forces of darkness. This is the type of peace that all men of goodwill hate. It is the type of peace that is obnoxious. It is the type of peace that stinks in the nostrils of the Almighty God.

Now let me hasten to say that this is not a concession to or a justification for physical war. I can see no moral justification for that type of war. I believe absolutely and positively that violence is self-defeating. War is devastating and we know now that if we continue to use these weapons of destruction, our civilization will be plunged across the abyss of destruction.

However, this is a type of war that every Christian is involved in. It is a spiritual war. It is a war of ideas. Every true Christian is a fighting pacifist.

In a very profound passage which has been often misunderstood, Jesus utters this: He says, "Think not that I am come to bring peace. I come not to bring peace but a sword." Certainly, He is not saying that He comes not to bring peace in the higher sense. What He is saying is: "I come not to bring this peace of escapism, this peace that fails to confront the real issues of life, the peace that makes for stagnant complacency." Then He says, "I come to bring a sword," but not a physical sword. Whenever I come, a conflict is precipitated between the old and the new, between justice and injustice, between the forces of light and the forces of darkness. I come to declare war over injustice. I come to declare war on evil. Peace is not merely the absence of some negative force—war, tension, confusion, but it is the presence of some positive force—justice, goodwill, the power of the kingdom of God.

I had a long talk with a man the other day about this bus situation. He discussed the peace being destroyed in the community, the destroying of good race relations. I agree that it is more tension now. But peace is not merely the absence of this tension, but the presence of justice. And even if we didn't have this tension, we still wouldn't have positive peace. Yes, it is true that if the Negro accepts his place, accepts exploitation and injustice, there will be peace. But it would be a peace boiled down to stagnant complacency, deadening passivity, and if peace means this, I don't want peace.

1) If peace means accepting second-class citizenship, I don't want it.

2) If peace means keeping my mouth shut in the midst of injustice and evil, I don't want it.

3) If peace means being complacently adjusted to a deadening status quo, I don't want peace.

4) If peace means a willingness to be exploited eco-
nomically, dominated politically, humiliated and
segregated, I don't want peace. So in a passive,
nonviolent manner, we must revolt against this
peace.

Jesus says in substance, I will not be content until justice,
goodwill, brotherhood, love, yes, the Kingdom of God are
established upon the earth. This is real peace—a peace
embodied with the presence of positive good. The inner
peace that comes as a result of doing God's will.

Together, You Can Redeem the Soul of Our Nation

John Lewis

While my time here has now come to an end, I want you to know that in the last days and hours of my life you inspired me. You filled me with hope about the next chapter of the great American story when you used your power to make a difference in our society. Millions of people motivated simply by human compassion laid down the burdens of division. Around the country and the world you set aside race, class, age, language and nationality to demand respect for human dignity.

That is why I had to visit Black Lives Matter Plaza in Washington, though I was admitted to the hospital the following day. I just had to see and feel it for myself that, after many years of silent witness, the truth is still marching on.

Lewis wrote this essay shortly before his death on July 17, 2020, to be published upon the day of his funeral, July 30, 2020.

Emmett Till was my George Floyd. He was my Rayshard Brooks, Sandra Bland and Breonna Taylor. He was 14 when he was killed, and I was only 15 years old at the time. I will never ever forget the moment when it became so clear that he could easily have been me. In those days, fear constrained us like an imaginary prison, and troubling thoughts of potential brutality committed for no understandable reason were the bars.

Though I was surrounded by two loving parents, plenty of brothers, sisters and cousins, their love could not protect me from the unholy oppression waiting just outside that family circle. Unchecked, unrestrained violence and government-sanctioned terror had the power to turn a simple stroll to the store for some Skittles or an innocent morning jog down a lonesome country road into a nightmare. If we are to survive as one unified nation, we must discover what so readily takes root in our hearts that could rob Mother Emanuel Church in South Carolina of her brightest and best, shoot unwitting concertgoers in Las Vegas and choke to death the hopes and dreams of a gifted violinist like Elijah McClain.

Like so many young people today, I was searching for a way out, or some might say a way in, and then I heard the voice of Dr. Martin Luther King Jr. on an old radio. He was talking about the philosophy and discipline of nonviolence. He said we are all complicit when we tolerate injustice. He said it is not enough to say it will get better by and by. He said each of us has a moral obligation to stand up, speak up and speak out. When you see something that is not right, you must say something. You must do something. Democracy is not a state. It is an act, and each generation must do its part to help build what we called the Beloved Community, a nation and world society at peace with itself.

Ordinary people with extraordinary vision can redeem the soul of America by getting in what I call good trouble, necessary trouble. Voting and participating in the democratic process are key. The vote is the most powerful nonviolent change agent you have in a democratic society. You must use it because it is not guaranteed. You can lose it.

You must also study and learn the lessons of history because humanity has been involved in this soul-wrenching, existential struggle for a very long time. People on every continent have stood in your shoes, through decades and centuries before you. The truth does not change, and that is why the answers worked out long ago can help you find solutions to the challenges of our time. Continue to build union between movements stretching across the globe because we must put away our willingness to profit from the exploitation of others.

Though I may not be here with you, I urge you to answer the highest calling of your heart and stand up for what you truly believe. In my life I have done all I can to demonstrate that the way of peace, the way of love and nonviolence is the more excellent way. Now it is your turn to let freedom ring.

When historians pick up their pens to write the story of the 21st century, let them say that it was your generation who laid down the heavy burdens of hate at last and that peace finally triumphed over violence, aggression and war. So I say to you, walk with the wind, brothers and sisters, and let the spirit of peace and the power of everlasting love be your guide.

Pause for Peace

God can't give us peace and happiness apart from Himself because there is no such thing.

—C. S. Lewis

Ultimately, we have just one moral duty: to reclaim large areas of peace in ourselves, more and more peace, and to reflect it towards others. And the more peace there is in us, the more peace there will also be in our troubled world.

—Etty Hillesum

The earth is too small a star and we too brief a visitor upon it for anything to matter more than the struggle for peace.

—Colman McCarthy

The Way of Peace

*Peace is the generous, tranquil contri-
bution of all to the good of all. Peace
is dynamism. Peace is generosity. It is
right and it is duty.*

—Óscar A. Romero

*Do your little bit of good where you
are; it's those little bits of good put together that overwhelm the world.*

—Desmond Tutu

*The fruit of silence is prayer, the fruit of
prayer is faith, the fruit of faith is love,
the fruit of love is service, and the fruit
of service is peace.*

—Mother Teresa

45

On the Pulse of Morning

Maya Angelou

Each of you, a bordered country,
Delicate and strangely made proud,
Yet thrusting perpetually under siege.
Your armed struggles for profit
Have left collars of waste upon
My shore, currents of debris upon my
        breast.
Yet, today I call you to my riverside,
If you will study war no more.

Come, clad in peace
and I will sing the songs
The Creator gave to me when I and
        the
Tree and the Rock were one.
Before cynicism was a bloody sear
        across your brow

and when you yet knew you still knew
      nothing
The River sings and sings on.

Imagine

John Lennon

Imagine there's no countries
It isn't hard to do
Nothing to kill or die for
And no religion, too
Imagine all the people
Living life in peace

PART THREE

PRAYERS FOR PEACE

It is better in prayer to have a heart without words than words without heart.

—MAHATMA GANDHI

In the Night of Weariness

Joyce Rupp

> *In the night of weariness, let me give*
> *myself up to sleep without struggle,*
> *resting my trust upon You.*
> —RABINDRANATH TAGORE,
> *THE HEART OF GOD*

When troubles arise, how quickly
struggle follows, giving full energy
to avoid, get rid of, resist, combat,
trying to change what is permanent.

Weary, weary the person who fights
against the steel beast of finality.
Peaceful the person wisely accepting
what cannot be changed or cured.

Rest the troubled mind on the pillow,
give the churning heart over to sleep;

be the wounded one cradled with love
in the open arms of a beloved presence.

Trust that however this life evolves
the Resilient One remains near,
a safe harbor offering shelter,
urging acceptance, providing hope.

48

A Prayer for Peace Within

Rebecca Barlow Jordan

When Confusion Reigns

O Lord, sometimes my insides feel like a battle zone, where missiles are falling too close to home. Other times I'm caught in an endless storm, with thoughts flying out of control. Confusion reigns, and defeat creeps in to steal my joy. I need your peace—the deep-down-in-your-heart kind that stays with me day and night and speaks confidently into the wind. Calm my anxious spirit, Lord; all the attacking "if-onlys" and "what-ifs" fill me with needless worry.

I know that trust is a big part of experiencing peace and that fear has no place in my life. Most of the things I worry about or dread don't even happen. So I'm declaring my trust in you. I'm releasing the reins of my life again and asking you to take control. I may need to pray this same prayer daily, but I'm tired of the frenzy of life that leaves my schedule and my thoughts without any margin. I need more of you, Lord, and less of me.

Finding Peace Within

I surrender and admit: I can't control people, plans, or even all my circumstances, but I can yield those things to you, and focus on your goodness. Thank you today for every good gift you've given, every blessing you've sent, all the forgiveness I did not deserve, and, yes, for every trial you've allowed into my life. You bring good out of every circumstance if I'll only let go and believe you. I know that when I pray and give thanks instead of worrying, you have promised that I can experience the kind of peace that passes all understanding. That's your kind of peace, Lord. And it's the kind I crave.

Whenever I'm stressed, anxious, or afraid, help me remember to run to you. You're the only one that can calm my fears and end my fretful behavior. Whether in trivial or heavy matters, I know you will not only give me peace; Lord, you will be my peace. And when I draw close to you—in prayer, in reading your Word, in helping another, in taking my mind off myself—you will be there, up close and personal.

I can't handle these times alone, Lord. Will you speak peace and calm my storms, or hold my hand while we walk through them together? Will you bring the reassuring wisdom of those who have come through similar times into my life? Thank you, Lord. I'm trusting you.

In the name of the One who makes the wind and the waves stand still, Amen.

49

Prayer for Peace (September 11)

Zalman Schachter-Shalomi

May the Holy One who blessed our
ancestors
and us over these many centuries,
helping us to get through the many
tragedies
and the great pain we have known,
bless all those whose lives
have been changed by this violence.
May those who witnessed these events
find reconciliation and an inner peace
which allows them to live without fear.
May those who suffered injury
find healing and recovery.
And may those who have lost loved
ones
find comfort and consolation

in the presence of family, friends, and
    community.
Our Mother, who is the source of our
    very being,
please gather the souls of those who
    passed on
in this tragedy under Your wings
and close to Your heart.
Keep them close to us who live on,
that they inspire us to seek peace,
to be peace, and to end the curse of
    killing,
hatred, and fear which blocks us
from becoming the compassionate be-
    ings
which You created us to be.
May the souls of those who were lost
    today
be bound up with those who live on
that we not forget the love they shared
and the love we all need to share.
May they rest in peace.
Amen.

50

Prayer for Peace

Pope Francis

Lord God of peace, hear our prayer!

We have tried so many times and over so many years to resolve our conflicts by our own powers and by the force of our arms. How many moments of hostility and darkness have we experienced; how much blood has been shed; how many lives have been shattered; how many hopes have been buried. . . . But our efforts have been in vain.

Now, Lord, come to our aid! Grant us peace, teach us peace; guide our steps in the way of peace. Open our eyes and our hearts, and give us the courage to say: "Never again war!"; "With war everything is lost." Instill in our hearts the courage to take concrete steps to achieve peace.

Lord, God of Abraham, God of the Prophets, God of Love, you created us and you call us to live as brothers and sisters. Give us the strength daily to be instruments of peace; enable us to see everyone who crosses our path as our brother or sister. Make us sensitive to the plea of our citizens who entreat us to turn our weapons of war into implements of peace, our trepidation into confident trust, and our quarreling into forgiveness.

Keep alive within us the flame of hope, so that with patience and perseverance we may opt for dialogue and reconciliation. In this way may peace triumph at last, and may the words "division," "hatred," and "war" be banished from the heart of every man and woman. Lord, defuse the violence of our tongues and our hands. Renew our hearts and minds, so that the word which always brings us together will be "brother," and our way of life will always be that of: Shalom, Peace, Salaam!

Amen.

51

Ecumenical Prayer for Peace

Hermann Schalück

O one God of all nations.
You created the earth and the cosmos,
in their differences, beauty and frailty.

The various cultures and religions seek
    You,
the origin of all things.
You want all to be for each other, not
    a threat,
but a blessing.

Our one world should be, by Your will,
an inhabitable and peaceful home.

You chose the Near East to make known
    to us all
Your Name and Your Path in many
    places.

Abraham, the Father in faith of Jews,
      Muslims and Christians,
listened to your appeal in the region
      between the
Euphrates and the Tigris, the present-
      day Iraq.

To the old and new People of Israel You
      promised
life and a future in a special way.

As Christian women and men, we thank
      You
especially for our Lord and Brother
      Jesus Christ.
He is our Peace.
He came to knock down walls and to
      give to all, without distinction,
life and a future.

We know ourselves to be in communion
      with the
Churches of the Near East.
They give testimony to the Gospel of
      Jesus,
to the liberating power of nonviolence
and to the certainty of the Resurrec-
      tion.

Hermann Schalück

We also pray to You
in unity with all the Brothers and Sis-
      ters of those Religions,
which have their origins in the Near
      East.

You created us all in Your own images
      and likeness,
we are Your image.
In all those that seek You in truth,
You have inspired hunger and thirst for
      justice
and a desire for peace.

All, Muslims, Christians and Members of
      the People of Israel,
earnestly aspire to reconciliation.

All are in mourning for the victims
of hatred and violence.
All, in accordance with Your project, are
      also called
to collaborate in the construction of a
      new world.

We, therefore, beseech You:
Have mercy on all the victims and on
      all the blameworthy.

The Way of Peace

Put an end to the spiral of violence, of
       enmity,
of hatred, of vendetta.

Give to all, especially to those responsible
       for politics,
the conviction that the way to lasting
       peace
is not that of war,
but of peace with justice.

Awaken in all the Religions
and in the people of today that they
       should be
instruments and messengers
of a different world.

Cause hearts to open and war to cease,
before it even begins.
Give lasting peace to the Near East.
Make a secure homeland a reality for
       all.

Lord, have all those of good will from all
       Religions,
in the North and South, in the East and
       West, in common responsibility,
to demolish the mountain of misunder-
       standing,

to fill in the trenches of hatred
and to make smooth the paths towards
    a common future.

Make the guns silent in our one world
and have, instead, the appeal for peace
    resound ever stronger,
for all, without distinction.
O Lord, the one God.

52

Prayer for the Morning Headlines

Daniel Berrigan

Mercifully grant peace in our days.

Through your help may we be freed from present distress.

Have mercy on women and children, homeless in foul
weather,

ranting like bees among gutted barns and stiles.

Have mercy on those (like us) clinging one to another
under fire.

Have mercy on the dead, befouled, trodden like snow in
hedges and thickets.

Have mercy, dead man, whose grandiose gentle hope died
on the wing,

whose body stood like a tree between strike and fall, stood
like a cripple on his wooden crutch.

We cry: Halt! We cry: Password!

Dishonored heart, remember and remind, the open sesame:

from there to here, from innocence to us:

Daniel Berrigan

Hiroshima Dresden Guernica Selma Sharpeville Coventry
   Dachau Vietnam Afghanistan Iraq.
Into our history, pass! Seed hope. Flower peace.

53

Prayer for Peace

Thomas Merton

Almighty and merciful God, Father of all men, Creator and Ruler of the Universe, Lord of History, whose designs are inscrutable, whose glory is without blemish, whose compassion for the errors of men is inexhaustible, in your will is our peace.

Mercifully hear this prayer which rises to you from the tumult and desperation of a world in which you are forgotten, in which your name is not invoked, your laws are derided, and your presence is ignored. Because we do not know you, we have no peace.

From the heart of an eternal silence, you have watched the rise of empires, and have seen the smoke of their downfall. You have seen Egypt, Assyria, Babylon, Greece, and Rome, once powerful, carried away like sand in the

---

This prayer was read in the House of Representatives on April 12, 1962.

wind. You have witnessed the impious fury of ten thousand fratricidal wars, in which great powers have torn whole continents to shreds in the name of peace and justice.

And now our nation itself stands in imminent danger of a war the like of which has never been seen! This nation dedicated to freedom, not to power, has obtained, through freedom, a power it did not desire. And seeking by that power to defend its freedom, it is enslaved by the process and policies of power. Must we wage a war we do not desire, a war that can do us no good, and which our very hatred of war forces us to prepare?

A day of ominous decision has now dawned on this free nation. Armed with a titanic weapon, and convinced of our own right, we face a powerful adversary, armed with the same weapon, equally convinced that he is right.

In this moment of destiny, this moment we never foresaw, we cannot afford to fail. Our choice of peace or war may decide our judgment and publish it in an eternal record. In this fatal moment of choice in which we might begin the patient architecture of peace, we may also take the last step across the rim of chaos.

Save us then from our obsessions! Open our eyes, dissipate confusions, teach us to understand ourselves and our adversary! Let us never forget that sins against the law of love are punished by loss of faith, and those without faith stop at no crime to achieve their ends!

Help us to be masters of the weapons that threaten to master us. Help us to use our science for peace and plenty, not for war and destruction. Show us how to use atomic power to bless our children's children, not to blight them. Save us from the compulsion to follow our adversaries in all that we most hate, confirming them in their hatred and suspicion of us.

Resolve our inner contradictions, which now grow beyond belief and beyond bearing. They are at once a torment and a blessing: for if you had not left us the light of conscience, we would not have to endure them. Teach us to be long-suffering in anguish and insecurity.

Teach us to wait and trust.

Grant light, grant strength and patience to all who work for peace. To this Congress, our President, our military forces, and our adversaries. Grant us prudence in proportion to our power,

Wisdom in proportion to our science, humaneness in proportion to our wealth and might. And bless our earnest will to help all races and people to travel, in friendship with us, along the road to justice, liberty, and lasting peace.

But grant us above all to see that our ways are not necessarily your ways, that we cannot fully penetrate the mystery of your designs and that the very storm of power now raging on this earth reveals your hidden will and your inscrutable decision.

Grant us to see your face in the lightning of this cosmic storm, O God of holiness, merciful to men: Grant us to seek peace where it is truly found! In your will, O God, is our peace!

A Prayer for America

Marianne Williamson

Dear God,
Please help us change America
from a land of violence
to a land of love.
Where there is separation,
please bring union.
Where there is distrust and pain,
please bring reconciliation of our hearts
with each other and with You.
May all be blessed
and prosper,
here and throughout the world.
And so it is.
Amen.

A Prayer for the World

Marianne Williamson

Dear God,

We pray for this our world.
We ask that You remove the walls that
      separate us and the chains that
      hold us down.
Use us to create a new world on earth,
      one that reflects Your will, Your
      vision, Your peace.
In this moment, we recognize the
      power You have given us to create
      anew the world we want.

Today's world, dear Lord, reflects our past
      confusion.
Now, in this moment, we ask for new
      light.
Illumine our minds.

Use us, dear Lord, as never before, as part
   of a great and mighty plan for the
   healing of this world.
May we no longer be at war with each
   other.
May we no longer be at war with
   ourselves.

Let us forgive this century and every
   other, evils of history, the pain of
   our common fears.
Remove from our hearts the illusion
   that we are separate.
May every nation and every people and
   every color and every religion
   find at last the one heartbeat we
   share,

Through You, our common Father/
   Mother and the redeemer of our
   broken dreams.
May we not hold onto yesterday.
May we not obscure Your vision of to-
   morrow but rather may You flood
   our hearts.

Flow through us, work through us, that
   in our lives we might be the illu-
   mined world.

Create, sustain that world on earth, dear
      God, for us and for our children.
Hallelujah, at the thought,

Praise God, the possibility that such a
      thing could come to be, through
      you, through
Your light that shines within us.

So may it be.
So may it be.

We thank you, Lord.

Amen.

A Christmas Prayer for Peace

John Dear

God of Peace,

Thank you for your Christmas gift of peace, for the birth and life of the nonviolent Jesus, and for all the blessings of peace, hope and love he offers.

Thank you for being a peaceful, nonviolent God. Thank you for blessing peacemakers, justice-seekers, the poor, the mournful, the meek, the pure of heart and children. Thank you for making the sun rise on the good and the bad and the rain to fall on the just and the unjust. Thank you for all the ways you work to end war, hunger, poverty and injustice. Thank you for all your hard work for the coming of peace on earth.

Thank you for showing us the way forward through the life, death and resurrection of the nonviolent Jesus. As we celebrate his birth and life, give us new grace, strength and energy to carry on his work of peace and nonviolence, that we might become his faithful disciples, apostles, companions and friends, that we might grow up and act like your beloved sons and daughters, that we might be your holy peacemakers.

This year, God of peace, help us to become more authentic people of Gospel nonviolence. Inspire millions of Christians around the world to reject violence and the just war theory once and for all and to understand and embrace the nonviolence of Jesus with a firm new commitment. May more and more of us take his nonviolence to heart and set about disarming ourselves, our church, our nations and our world.

May every Christian renounce violence, stop hurting others, get rid of their guns, quit the military, refuse to join the military, teach nonviolence, join the grassroots movements of nonviolence, work publicly for justice and disarmament, and make the nonviolence of Jesus central in our lives, as Gandhi, Martin Luther King Jr. and Dorothy Day did.

Help us create new social movements of Gospel nonviolence to speed up the abolition of war, poverty, nuclear weapons and environmental destruction. Help bring your vision of a nonviolent world into the mainstream, that everyone may seek that higher way of life.

Bless our efforts to raise up nonviolence publicly, to promote disarmament and justice, and to help heal humanity. Inspire more and more people to discuss how they can become more nonviolent. Help us take to the streets to say a public nonviolent "No!" to gun violence, war, corporate greed, drones, killings, NSA surveillance, starvation, systemic injustice, nuclear weapons and catastrophic climate change, that we might promote real institutional, political change for disarmament and justice and end the violence.

Help us to take personally the prayer of Zechariah, the father of John the Baptist, that we too might prepare a way for you: "You will be called 'prophet of the most high,' for you will go before the God of peace to prepare God's ways, to give God's people knowledge of salvation through the forgiveness of their sins, because of the tender mercy of our God by which the daybreak from on high will visit us to shine on those who sit in darkness and death's shadow, to guide our feet into the path of peace."

Through the example of the nonviolent Jesus, help us to walk the path of peace, proclaim your vision of peace and welcome your Christmas gift of peace on earth.

This Christmas, make us as nonviolent as Jesus.

We ask this in the name of the nonviolent Jesus. Amen.

A Prayer from Apollo 8 for Universal Justice

Frank Borman

Give us, O God, the vision which can
    see Your love in the world in spite
    of human failure.
Give us the faith to trust Your good-
    ness in spite of our ignorance and
    weakness.

Give us the knowledge that we may
    continue to pray with understand-
    ing hearts.
And show us what each one of us can
    do to set forward the coming of
    the day of universal peace.

The Disturbing Peace of Christ

Joseph R. Veneroso

May the peace of Christ disturb you
And shake you from your dreams
To see the reality of life all around you.

Despite the storms of war and violence
Amid tears and bitterness
Remember: from the cross of earthly
    defeat
Christ prayed divine forgiveness upon
Our ungrateful and indifferent world
Whose fragile and illusory peace
Comes from overpowering our
    enemies.

No, the shalom of Christ takes root
    and rules

In the heart that refuses to hate
In the mind that seeks true justice
On the lips that bless, not curse
In the soul aware of its utter
      dependence
On God's abundant mercy.

Only Christ's peace brings blessed
      assurance
That despite setbacks, failures,
      disappointment
And defeat and amid physical hardship
      and
Discouragement while wandering
In the wilderness of uncertainty
Not only are we exactly where
God wants us to be
But Jesus himself is with us in the
      struggle.

59

A Prayer for Inner Peace

Unknown

Lord, please put Your peace in my heart.
I'm worried and anxious.
My mind races and obsesses.
I can't help thinking about my prob-
    lems.
And the more I think about them, the
    more depressed I become.
I feel like I'm sinking down in quick-
    sand and can't get out.
Calm me, Lord.
Slow me down, put Your peace in my
    heart.

No matter what problem I have, Lord,
You are bigger, You are more powerful
    than it is.
So I bring my problem to You.
I know what I want.

I know my will.

I do not know Yours.

I do not know how You will use this
problem for my salvation.

I do not know what good You will
work out from this evil.

But I trust You.

I trust Your goodness and Your wisdom.

So I place myself in Your hands.

Please fill my heart with peace.

60

Deep Peace

Fiona Macleod

Deep peace I breathe into you,
O weariness, here:
O ache, here!
Deep peace, a soft white dove to you;
Deep peace, a quiet rain to you;
Deep peace, an ebbing wave to you!
Deep peace, red wind of the east from you;
Deep peace, grey wind of the west to you;
Deep peace, dark wind of the north from you;
Deep peace, blue wind of the south to you!
Deep peace, pure red of the flame to you;
Deep peace, pure white of the moon to you;
Deep peace, pure green of the grass to you;
Deep peace, pure brown of the earth to you;
Deep peace, pure grey of the dew to you,
Deep peace, pure blue of the sky to you!
Deep peace of the running wave to you,
Deep peace of the flowing air to you,

Deep peace of the quiet earth to you,
Deep peace of the sleeping stones to you!
Deep peace of the Yellow Shepherd to you,
Deep peace of the Wandering Shepherdess to
    you,
Deep peace of the Flock of Stars to you,
Deep peace from the Son of Peace to you,
Deep peace from the heart of Mary to you,
And from Briget of the Mantle
Deep peace, deep peace!
And with the kindness too of the Haughty
    Father
Peace!
In the name of the Three who are One,
Peace! And by the will of the King of the
    Elements,
Peace! Peace!

61

Interfaith Prayers

Unknown

Baha'i Prayer for Peace

Be generous in prosperity, and thankful in adversity.
Be fair in thy judgment, and guarded in thy speech.
Be a lamp unto those who walk in darkness, and a
home to the stranger.
Be eyes to the blind, and a guiding light unto the
feet of the erring.
Be a breath of life to the body of humankind, a dew
to the soil of the human heart,
and a fruit upon the tree of humility.

Buddhist Prayer for Peace

May all beings everywhere plagued with
sufferings of body and mind

quickly be freed from their illnesses.
May those frightened cease to be afraid, and
may those bound be free.
May the powerless find power, and may
people think of befriending one another.
May those who find themselves in trackless,
fearful wildernesses—
the children, the aged, the unprotected—
be guarded by beneficent celestials,
and may they swiftly attain Buddhahood.

Beatitudes

Christian Prayer for Peace

Blessed are the Peacemakers, for they shall be known as
the Children of God.
But I say to you that hear, love your enemies, do good to
those who hate you,
bless those who curse you, pray for those who abuse you.
To those who strike you on the cheek, offer the other also,
and from those who take away your cloak, do not withhold
your coat as well.
Give to everyone who begs from you,
and of those who take away your goods, do not ask them
again.
And as you wish that others would do to you, do so to them.

Unknown

Hindu Prayers for Peace

O God, lead us from the unreal to the Real.
O God, lead us from darkness to light.
O God, lead us from death to immortality.
Shanti, Shanti, Shanti unto all.
O Lord God almighty, may there be peace in
celestial regions.
May there be peace on earth.
May the waters be appeasing.
May herbs be wholesome, and may trees and
plants bring peace to all.
May all beneficent beings bring peace to us.
May thy Vedic Law propagate peace all
through the world.
May all things be a source of peace to us.
And may thy peace itself, bestow peace on all,
and may that peace come to me also.

Jewish Prayer for Peace

Come let us go up to the mountain of the Lord,
that we may walk the paths of the Most High.
And we shall beat our swords into ploughshares,
and our spears into pruning hooks.
Nation shall not lift up sword against nation—

neither shall they learn war any more.
And none shall be afraid,
for the mouth of the Lord of Hosts has spoken.

Muslim Prayer for Peace

In the name of Allah, the beneficent, the merciful.
Praise be to the Lord of the Universe
who has created us and made us into tribes and nations,
that we may know each other,
not that we may despise each other.
If the enemy incline towards peace,
do thou also incline towards peace, and trust in God,
for the Lord is the one that heareth and knoweth all things.
And the servants of God,
Most Gracious are those who walk on the Earth in humility,
and when we address them,
we say "PEACE."

Native African Prayer for Peace

Almighty God, the Great Thumb we cannot
evade to tie any knot;
the Roaring Thunder that splits mighty trees:
the all-seeing Lord up on high who sees even

the footprints
of an antelope on a rockmass here on Earth.
You are the one who does not hesitate to
respond to our call.
You are the cornerstone of peace.

Native American Prayer for Peace

O Great Spirit of our Ancestors, I raise my pipe
to you.
To your messengers the four winds,
and to Mother Earth who provides for your
children.
Give us the wisdom to teach our children to
love, to respect,
and to be kind to each other so that they may
grow with peace in mind.
Let us learn to share all the good things you
provide for us on this Earth.

Shinto Prayer for Peace

Although the people living across the ocean surrounding us,
I believe, are all our brothers and sisters,
why are there constant troubles in this world?

Why do winds and waves rise in the ocean surrounding us?
I only earnestly wish that the wind will soon puff away
all the clouds which are hanging over the tops of the
mountains.

Sikh Prayers for Peace

God adjudges us according to our deeds, not the coat that
we wear:
that Truth is above everything, but higher still is truthful
living.
Know that we attaineth God when we loveth,
and only that victory endures in consequence of which
no one is defeated.
Know that we attain God when we love,
and only that victory endures in consequence of which
no one is defeated.

Sufi Prayer for Peace

O Almighty Sun, whose light clears away all clouds,
We take refuge in you. Guide of all people, God of all dei-
ties, Lord of all angels,
We pray you to dispel the mists of illusion from the hearts
of the nations

Unknown

And lift their lives by your all-sufficient power,
Your ever shining light, your everlasting life,
Your heavenly joy and your perfect peace.

A Time for Peace

Ecclesiastes 3:1–8

For everything there is a season,
and a time for every matter under heaven:
a time to be born, and a time to die;
a time to plant, and a time to pluck up
what is planted;
a time to kill, and a time to heal;
a time to break down, and a time to build up;
a time to weep, and a time to laugh;
a time to mourn, and a time to dance;
a time to throw away stones, and a time to
gather stones together;
a time to embrace, and a time to
refrain from embracing;
a time to seek, and a time to lose;
a time to keep, and a time to throw away;
a time to tear, and a time to sew;
a time to keep silence, and a time to speak;
a time to love, and a time to hate;
a time for war, and a time for peace. . . .

Psalm 23

Norman Fischer translation

You are my shepherd, I am content
You lead me to rest in the sweet grasses
To lie down by the quiet waters
And I am refreshed

You lead me down the right path
The path that unwinds in the pattern of your
    name
And even if I walk through the valley of the
    shadow of death
I will not fear
For you are with me
Comforting me with your rod and your staff

Showing me each step
You prepare a table for me
In the midst of my adversity
And moisten my head with oil

Surely my cup is overflowing
And goodness and kindness will follow me
All the days of my life
And in the long days beyond
I will always live in your house

The Serenity Prayer

Reinhold Niebuhr

God, grant me the serenity
to accept the things I cannot change,
courage to change the things I can,
and wisdom to know the difference;

living one day at a time,
enjoying one moment at a time;
accepting hardships as a pathway to peace;
taking, as Jesus did, this sinful world as it is,
not as I would have it;
trusting that You will make all things right
if I surrender to Your will;

so that I may be reasonably happy in this life
and supremely happy with You forever in the
next.

The Peace Prayer
of Saint Francis

Lord, make me an instrument of your peace.
Where there is hatred, let me show love,
Where there is injury, pardon
Where there is doubt, faith,
Where there is despair, hope,
Where there is darkness, light,
Where there is sadness, joy.
O Divine Master, grant that I may not so
        much seek to be consoled as to console
Not so much to be understood as to under-
        stand
Not so much to be loved, as to love;
For it is in giving that we receive,
It is in pardoning that we are pardoned,
It is in dying that we awake to eternal life.

Let There Be Peace on Earth

Jill Jackson-Miller
and Sy Miller

Let there be peace on earth
And let it begin with me

Let there be peace on Earth
The peace that was meant to be

With God as our Father
Brothers all are we

Let me walk with my brother
In perfect harmony.

Let peace begin with me
Let this be the moment now.

The Way of Peace

With ev'ry step I take
Let this be my solemn vow

To take each moment and live
Each moment in peace eternally

Let there be peace on earth
And let it begin with me.

Sources and Acknowledgments

Orbis Books has made every effort to identify the owner of each selection in this book, and to obtain permission from the author, publisher, or agent in question. In the event of inadvertent errors, please notify us.

1. Unknown, "Perfect Peace." http://www.skywriting.net/ inspirational/stories/perfect_peace.html.

2. David Steindl-Rast, OSB, and Sharon Lebell. "The Music of Silence." From *The Music of Silence: Entering the Sacred Space of Monastic Experience*, copyright © 1995 by David Steindl-Rast and Sharon Lebell. Used by permission of HarperCollins Publishers. Reprinted in Frederic and Mary Ann Brussat, *Spiritual Literacy: Reading the Sacred in Everyday Life* (New York: Touchstone, 1996).

3. Deepak Chopra, "Seven Practices for Peace." From "The Way of Peace," *Peace Is the Way: Bringing War and Violence to an End* by Deepak Chopra, copyright © 2005 by Deepak Chopra. Used by permission of Harmony Books, an imprint of Random House, a division of Penguin Random House LLC. All rights reserved.

4. Thomas Merton, "There Are No Strangers." From *Conjectures of a Guilty Bystander*, copyright © 1965, 1966 by The Abbey of Gethsemani. Used by permission of Doubleday, an imprint of the Knopf Doubleday Publishing Group, a division of Penguin Random House LLC. All rights reserved.

5. Pema Chödrön, "Pause Practice." From "Take Three Conscious Breaths." *Lion's Roar* online, April 2, 2017, https:// www.lionsroar.com/take-three-conscious-breaths/.

6. John Dear, "A Mindfulness Walk in Peace," *National Catholic Reporter* online, October 23, 2012, https://www.ncronline. Reprinted by permission of John Dear.

7. Thich Nhat Hanh, "The Miracle Is to Walk on Earth." From *Touching Peace: Practicing the Art of Mindful Living* (Berkeley, CA: Parallax Press, 1992). Used by permission.

8. Michael Leach, "Dandelions." From *Why Stay Catholic* (Chicago: Loyola Press, 2011). Copyright © Michael Leach. Reprinted with permission of Loyola Press. To order copies visit www.loyolapress.com.

9. Dom Hélder Câmara, "Trees, Sister Trees." From *Sister Earth* (Hyde Park, NY: New City Press, 1990), 103–5. Used by permission.

10. Wendell Berry, "The Peace of Wild Things." From *The Selected Poems of Wendell Berry*, copyright © 1998 by Wendell Berry. Reprinted by permission of Counterpoint Press.

11. Joan Chittister, "The Cave of the Heart." From *For Everything a Season* (Maryknoll, NY: Orbis Books, 2013), 147–52.

12. "There Is a Place in You." From *A Course in Miracles* ch. 29, pt. VI, v. 31.

13. Henri J. M. Nouwen, "Peace in the World Cannot Be Made without Peace in the Heart." From *The Road to Peace*, ed. John Dear (Maryknoll, NY: Orbis Books, 1998), 24–25.

14. Amy Eilberg, "Pray for Peace." From *From Enemy to Friend: Jewish Wisdom and the Pursuit of Peace* (Maryknoll, NY: Orbis Books, 2014), 263–66.

15. Robert V. Taylor, "Peace Within through *Ubuntu*." Copyright © Robert V. Taylor, www.robertvtaylor.com.

16. Michael Leach, "Nothing Can Separate Us from the Love of God." Adapted from *Why Stay Catholic* (Chicago: Loyola Press, 2011). Copyright © Michael Leach. Reprinted with permission of Loyola Press. To order copies visit www.loyola-press.com.

17. Sister Annabel Laity, "The Bell." From *Mindfulness: Walking with Jesus and Buddha* (Maryknoll, NY: Orbis Books, 2021).

18. Doug Crandall, "The Be It Poem." From *The Edge* online, May 1, 2007, https://www.edgemagazine.net/2007/05/the-be-it-poem/. Reprinted by permission of Doug Crandall and *The Edge*.

19. "Love Your Enemies." From Matthew 5:38–48.

Sources and Acknowledgments

20. Pope Benedict XVI, "The Magna Carta of Christian Non-violence." From *Angelus*, February 18, 2007. Copyright © Libreria Editrice Vaticana. Used by permission.

21. Pope Francis, "The Good News." From *Message of His Holiness Pope Francis for the Celebration of the Fiftieth World Day of Peace*, "Nonviolence: A Style of Politics for Peace," January 1, 2017. Copyright © Libreria Editrice Vaticana. Used by permission.

22. Riva Maendel, "It Starts with Us." From *Maryknoll Magazine*, May 1, 2017, https://www.maryknollmagazine.org/2018/05/essay-winners-2017-nonviolence/.

23. Clarence Jordan, "Blessed Are the Peacemakers." From *Sermon on the Mount* by Clarence Jordan, copyright © 1952 by Judson Press. Used by permission of Judson Press.

24. Mohandas Gandhi, "The Eternal Law of Love." From *The Collected Works of Mahatma Gandhi,* vol. 68, January 2, 1939, Ahmedabad: Navajivan Pub., 1967–84.

25. Terrence J. Rynne, "Gandhi and Jesus and Nonviolent Love." From *Gandhi and Jesus: The Saving Power of Nonviolence* (Maryknoll, NY: Orbis Books, 2008), 1–2, 186.

26. Greg Darr, "Honoring George Floyd on 38th & Chicago." From *Maryknoll Magazine*, June 8, 2020, https://www.maryknollmagazine.org/2020/06/remembering-george-floyd-38th-chicago/.

27. Michelle Obama, "It's Up to All of Us." From a May 30, 2020, Instagram statement following the death of George Floyd.

28. Rivera Sun, "Bullets Don't Have No Names." From "Know Your Nonviolent History—August 20, 2013, Antoinette Tuff Stopped a School Shooter with Nonviolence," August 18, 2016, www.riverasun.com. Copyright 2016 by Rivera Sun. Reprinted with permission of the author. Originally published in Pace e Bene's nonviolent history series, part of *This Nonviolent Life*.

29. Sojourner Truth, "Ain't I a Woman." From the published version of an address given at the Women's Rights Convention in Akron, Ohio, May 29, 1851, *Narrative of Sojourner Truth* (Boston, 1875).

30. Dorothy Day, "Love Is the Answer." From *Selected Writings* (Maryknoll, NY: Orbis Books, 1983), 337–39.

31. Joan Chittister, "My Enemy Has Become My Friend." From "Proceeding in the Ways of Peace Means Meeting Those We Fear, Those We Hate," *National Catholic Reporter*, July 8, 2003. Reprinted by permission of Joan Chittister.

32. Susanne Guenther Loewen, "Abigail the Peacemaker." From *Canadian Mennonite*, June 19, 2015, https://canadianmennonite.org/blogs/susie-guenther-loewen/abigail-peacemaker. Reprinted by permission of *Canadian Mennonite* and Susanne Guenther Loewen.

33. Francine Dempsey, "Construct No Walls around 'Sacred Space.'" From *National Catholic Reporter*, September 5, 2017. Reprinted by permission of Francine Dempsey.

34. Robert Ellsberg, "Peace Pilgrim." From *Blessed among All Women: Women Saints, Prophets, and Witnesses for Our Time* (New York: Crossroad, 2005), 255–57.

35. Peace Pilgrim, "What We Dwell Upon Happens." From *Peace Pilgrim: Her Life and Work in Her Own Words*, 2nd ed. (Santa Fe, NM: Ocean Tree Books, 1992), 99. Reprinted by permission.

36. Magda Yoors-Peeters, "Daring to Be Human," in *Peace Is the Way: Writings on Nonviolence from the Fellowship of Reconciliation,* ed. Walter Wink (Maryknoll, NY: Orbis Books, 2000), 258–59.

37. Cindy Brandt, "Peace, Peace. But for Whom?" From *Sojourners*, December 1, 2014. Used by permission of Cindy Brandt.

38. Megan McKenna, "Planting Seeds." From *Parables: The Arrows of God* (Maryknoll, NY: Orbis Books, 1994), 28–29.

39. Parker J. Palmer, "The Call of Conscience." From *The Active Life: A Spirituality of Work, Creativity, and Caring*, copyright © 1990 by Parker J. Palmer. Used by permission of HarperCollins Publishers. Reprinted in Frederic and Mary Ann Brussat, *Spiritual Literacy: Reading the Sacred in Everyday Life* (New York: Touchstone, 1996).

40. Martin Sheen, "What We Are Asked to Do." From his acceptance speech for the Notre Dame Laetare Medal Award, May 17, 2008.

41. Barack Obama, "Reach for the World That Ought to Be." From the Nobel Lecture by Barack H. Obama, Oslo, 10 December 2009. © The Nobel Foundation. Reprinted with permission.

42. Thomas Merton, "No Man Is an Island." From "Preface to the Vietnamese edition of *No Man Is an Island*," *"Honorable Reader": Reflections on My Work*, ed. Robert E. Daggy (New York: Crossroad, 1989), 123–26.

43. Martin Luther King Jr., "When Peace Becomes Obnoxious." Address given at Dexter Avenue Baptist Church, Montgomery, Ala., on March 18, 1956. Reprinted by arrangement with The Heirs to the Estate of Martin Luther King Jr., c/o Writers House as agent for the proprietor New York, NY. Copyright © 1956 by Dr. Martin Luther King Jr. Renewed © 1984 by Coretta Scott King.

44. John Lewis, "Together, You Can Redeem the Soul of Our Nation." From *The New York Times*, July 30, 2020. Copyright © 2020 The New York Times Company. All rights reserved. Used under license.

45. Maya Angelou, "On the Pulse of Morning," from *On the Pulse of Morning*, copyright © 1993 by Maya Angelou. Used by permission of Random House, an imprint and division of Penguin Random House LLC. All rights reserved.

46. John Lennon, "Imagine," Apple Records, September 9, 1971. Lennon described "Imagine" as "an ad campaign for peace." Written in March 1971, during the Vietnam war, it has become a permanent protest song and a lasting emblem of hope.

47. Joyce Rupp, "In the Night of Weariness." Original prayer written for this collection. Copyright © 2021 by Joyce Rupp.

48. Rebecca Barlow Jordan, "A Prayer for Peace Within." Copyright © 2015, Rebecca Barlow Jordan. https://www.rebeccabarlowjordan.com/prayer-for-peace. Used by permission. All rights reserved. First published on https://www.crosswalk.com.

49. Rabbi Zalman Schachter-Shalomi, "Prayer for Peace." From *All Breathing Life Adores Your Name*, ed. Michael L. Kagan. Gaon Books. Reprinted with permission of Gaon Books.

50. Pope Francis, "Prayer for Peace." Copyright © Libreria Editrice Vaticana. Used by permission.

51. Hermann Schalück, OFM, "Ecumenical Prayer for Peace." https://osfphila.org/spiritualityprayer/prayers-for-our-troops/ecumenical-prayer-for-peace/.

52. Daniel Berrigan, "Prayer for the Morning Headlines." From *Prayer for the Morning Headlines: On the Sanctity of Life and Death* (Baltimore, MD: Loyola University, Apprentice House Press, 2008). Used by permission.

53. Thomas Merton, "Prayer for Peace." From *Passion for Peace: The Social Essays*, ed. William H. Shannon (New York: Crossroad, 1995), 327–29.

54. Marianne Williamson, "A Prayer for America." From *The Healing of America* by Marianne Williamson. Copyright © 1997 by Marianne Williamson. Reprinted with the permission of Simon & Schuster, Inc. All rights reserved.

55. Marianne Williamson, "A Prayer for the World." From *Illuminata: Thoughts, Prayers, Rites of Passage* by Marianne Williamson. Copyright © 1994 by Marianne Williamson. Used by permission of Random House, an imprint and division of Penguin Random House LLC. All rights reserved.

56. John Dear, "A Christmas Prayer for Peace." From *National Catholic Reporter* online, December 24, 2013, https://www.ncronline.org/blogs/road-peace/christmas-prayer-peace-2. Reprinted by permission of John Dear.

57. Frank Borman, "A Prayer from Apollo 8 for Universal Justice." https://www.xavier.edu/jesuitresource/online-resources/prayer-index/justice-prayers.

58. Joseph R. Veneroso, MM, "The Disturbing Peace of Christ." From *Maryknoll Magazine*, January/February 2017, https://www.maryknollmagazine.org/reflections/886-2/.

59. Unknown, "A Prayer for Inner Peace." https://www.catholic-doors.com/prayers/english4/p02936.htm.

60. Fiona Macleod, "Deep Peace." From *The Dominion of Dreams: Under the Dark Star*. Copyright © Fiona Macleod (William Sharp, 1895).

Sources and Acknowledgments

61. Interfaith Mission Service, "Interfaith Prayers for Peace." http://www.interfaithmissionservice.org/wp-content/uploads/2012/02/Interfaith-Prayers-of-Peace.pdf.

62. "A Time for Peace," Ecclesiastes 3:1–8.

63. "Psalm 23," Norman Fischer translation. From *Opening to You: Zen Inspired Translations of the Psalms* (New York: Penguin Putnam, 2002). Used by permission.

64. Reinhold Niebuhr, "The Serenity Prayer."

65. "The Peace Prayer of St. Francis."

66. Jill Jackson-Miller and Sy Miller, "Let There Be Peace on Earth." Copyright 1955, 1983 by Jan-Lee Music (ASCAP). Reprinted by Permission. All Rights Reserved. International copyright secured.

Index of Contributors

Index of Contributors

Index of Contributors